Passing the APM Introductory Certificate
APMBOK 6 Edition

Robin Kay BA MBA

Copyright © 2014 by R.J.Kay.

robinjohnkay@aol.com

All rights reserved. No part of this publication may be reproduced, stored in a retrieval system, transmitted or utilised in any form or by any means, electronic, mechanical, photocopying, recording or otherwise without written permission from the author.

ISBN: 978-1-291-75051-5

Preface

The information contained within this book is based upon sound and generally accepted project management principals. It is intended to cover those areas of the APM Body of Knowledge (6th edition, 2013) that are included in the APM Introductory certificate syllabus.

To study for this certificate requires no prior knowledge or experience in project management. It is designed for anyone starting out on the first steps of a career in project management or those simply working in or around a project environment and who need to know a little more about project management.

There are two ways you can register to sit the APM Introductory Certificate: by registering for a training course and exam with an accredited training provider, or by self-study and sitting the exam on one of APM's open events.

Assessment is by a 60 question, multiple-choice exam taken over one hour

For more information see http://www.apm.org.uk/IntroductoryCertificate.asp

Contents

1 Project Management and the Operating Environment 7
    1.1 What is a project? 8
    1.2 Projects v Operations (Business as usual) 8
    1.3 The Key Purpose of Project Management 9
    1.4 The Core Components of Project Management 9
    1.5 The Benefits of Project Management 10
    1.6 Programme Management 10
        1.6.1 Benefits of Programme Management 11
        1.6.2 Programme Manager Roles & Responsibilities 11
    1.7 Portfolio Management 11
        1.7.1 Benefits of managing groups of projects as a portfolio 12
        1.7.2 Key Differences Between Programmes and Portfolios 13
    1.8 The Project Management Triangle 13
    1.9 Project Environment (Context) 14
    1.10 Environmental Impact Analysis (EIA) 14

2 Project Life Cycles and Reviews 17
    2.1 A Generic Lifecycle 18
    2.2 The Extended Project Life Cycle 18
    2.3 Benefits of Phasing 19
    2.4 Project Reviews 19
        2.4.1 Phase, Stage or Gate reviews 19
        2.4.2 Project Status reviews 20
        2.4.3 Project Audits 20
        2.4.4 Post Project Review/Lessons Learned Review 20
        2.4.5 Benefits Realisation review/Post Implementation review 20
        2.4.6 Peer Reviews 20
    2.5 Handover 21
        2.5.1 A Handover Process 21
    2.6 Closeout 21
    2.7 Post Project Review 22
        2.7.1 Agenda 22
        2.7.2 Planning considerations 22

3 Roles and responsibilities 23
    3.1 The Project Manager 24
    3.2 Project Organisation Structure 24
    3.3 The Project Board 25
    3.4 The Project Sponsor 25
        3.4.1 Sponsor responsibilities 25
        3.4.2 Sponsor activities 25
    3.5 The Project Team & Team Leaders 26
    3.6 The End Users 26
    3.7 Quality Assurance 26

- 3.8 The Project Office 26
  - 3.8.1 Project Support Office-PSO 27
  - 3.8.2 Project Management Office-PMO 27
  - 3.8.3 Enterprise Programme Management Office-EPMO 27
  - 3.8.4 Benefits of a Project Office...28
- 4 Project Management Planning 29
  - 4.1 Building the Business Case 30
    - 4.1.1 Business Case Objective & Purpose 30
    - 4.1.2 Contents of a Business Case 30
    - 4.1.3 Constructing a Business Case 30
    - 4.1.4 Key Contributors to the Business Case..31
  - 4.2 Success and Benefits Management 32
    - 4.2.1 Project Success Criteria 32
    - 4.2.2 Project Success Factors..32
    - 4.2.3 Key Performance Indicators 33
    - 4.2.4 Project Failure 33
  - 4.3 Stakeholder Management..33
    - 4.3.1 Typical Stakeholders..33
    - 4.3.2 The Stakeholder Management Process 34
    - 4.3.3 Benefits of Stakeholder Management 36
  - 4.4 The Project Management Plan 36
    - 4.4.1 The seven fundamental questions 36
    - 4.4.2 Project Plan Content 37
  - 4.5 Benefits of Planning 38
  - 4.6 Ownership, Authorship and Audience 38
  - 4.7 Benefits Management..38
    - 4.7.1 Responsibility 38
    - 4.7.2 Benefits review 39
  - 4.8 Estimating Methods...39
    - 4.8.1 Analytical (Bottom Up) Estimating 39
    - 4.8.2 Comparative Estimating...39
    - 4.8.3 Parametric Estimating..39
    - 4.8.4 The Estimating Funnel 40
  - 4.9 Project Reporting...41
    - 4.9.1 Report Structure 41
- 5 Scope Management...43
  - 5.1 Definition of Scope 44
  - 5.2 Work Breakdown Structure...44
    - 5.2.1 Benefits of the WBS 45
  - 5.3 The Product Breakdown Structure 45
  - 5.4 Relationship between WBS and PBS..46
  - 5.5 Cost Breakdown Structure 47
  - 5.6 Organisational Breakdown Structure (OBS)...47
  - 5.7 Responsibility Assignment Matrix (RAM) 48

- 5.8 Change Control 48
  - 5.8.1 Definition of a Change 48
  - 5.8.2 Why Change Control is Important 49
  - 5.8.3 The Change Control Process 49
  - 5.8.4 The Change Request Form 50
  - 5.8.5 Impact Assessment 50
  - 5.8.6 The Change Control Log 51
- 5.9 Configuration Management 51
  - 5.9.1 Configuration Management Activities 51
  - 5.9.2 Components of the Configuration Management System 52
  - 5.9.3 Link to change control 52
- 6 Scheduling & Resource Management 53
  - 6.1 The Precedence Diagramming Method 54
    - 6.1.1 Other Link Types & Leads and Lags 54
    - 6.1.2 Critical Path Analysis (CPA) 55
    - 6.1.3 Node Convention 55
    - 6.1.4 Worked Example 56
    - 6.1.5 The Critical Path 58
    - 6.1.6 Total Float and Free Float 58
    - 6.1.7 Gantt Charts 59
    - 6.1.8 Gantt Chart Features 59
    - 6.1.9 Gantt v Network 60
    - 6.1.10 Milestone Planning 60
    - 6.1.11 Baselines 60
  - 6.2 Resource Management 61
  - 6.3 Resource Smoothing 61
  - 6.4 Resource Levelling 62
  - 6.5 Procurement 63
    - 6.5.1 Definitions 63
    - 6.5.2 The Procurement Process 63
    - 6.5.3 Procurement Strategy 64
    - 6.5.4 Make or Buy 64
- 7 Project Risk & Issue Management 65
  - 7.1 Definitions of Risk 66
  - 7.2 The Risk Management Plan 66
  - 7.3 Risk Management Process 66
    - 7.3.1 Initiation 67
    - 7.3.2 Risk Identification 67
    - 7.3.3 Risk Assessment 68
    - 7.3.4 Risk Response Planning 69
    - 7.3.5 Implement Responses 70
    - 7.3.6 The Benefits of Managing Risk 71
    - 7.3.7 Drawbacks of Managing Risk 71
  - 7.4 Issue Management 71

- 7.4.1 Issue Log 72
8 Project Quality Management 73
  8.1 Definition of Quality 74
    8.1.1 Quality V Grade 74
    8.1.2 Elements of Quality Management 74
    8.1.3 Quality Planning 74
    8.1.4 Quality Assurance 75
    8.1.5 Quality Control 75
    8.1.6 Quality Control v Quality Assurance 75
    8.1.7 Continuous Improvement 75
    8.1.8 Project Management Responsibilities 76
9 Communication 77
  9.1 Communications Management 78
  9.2 Channels of Communication 78
  9.3 Barriers to Communication 79
    9.3.1 Environmental Barriers 79
    9.3.2 Background 79
    9.3.3 Personal 79
    9.3.4 Organisational 79
  9.4 Effective Communications 80
  9.5 Importance of effective communications planning 80
  9.6 The Communications Management Plan 80
10 Teamwork and Leadership 83
  10.1 The Project Manager as Leader 84
    10.1.1 Attributes of Good Leaders 84
    10.1.2 Leadership Activities 84
    10.1.3 Leadership Styles (Hersey & Blanchard) 85
  10.2 The Project Team 86
    10.2.1 A Team Definition 86
    10.2.2 Characteristics of Effective Teams 86
  10.3 Team models 86
    10.3.1 Belbin Roles 86
    10.3.2 Advantages & disadvantages 88
  10.4 Team Building 88
  10.5 Stages in Team Development 89
  10.6 Effective Team Building 90
11 Practice Questions 91
12 Practice Questions Answers 97

1 Project Management and the Operating Environment

Learning Objectives

- Define "what is a project" and "what is project management" and the key purpose of project management

- Be able to state the core components of project management

- Understand the benefits of effective project management

- Identify the differences between projects and business as usual

- Define the terms 'Programme Management' and 'Portfolio Management'

- Define the relationship between Time, Cost and Quality

- Understand what is meant by "project environment".

- Explain "PESTLE"

1.1   What is a project?

Here are three different definitions

"An endeavour in which human, material and financial resources are organised in a novel way to deliver a unique scope of work of given specification, often within constraints of cost and time, and to achieve beneficial change defined by quantitative and qualitative objectives."

The Association for Project Management

"A temporary endeavour undertaken to create a unique product, service or result."

Project Management Institute

A unique set of coordinated activities, with definite starting and finishing points, undertaken by an individual or organisation to meet specific objectives within defined schedule, cost and performance parameters"

BS6079 (Guide to Project Management)

All of these are valid definitions from which we can determine the following key characteristics that together differentiate projects from "business as usual".

- Projects are Unique. When doing a project we create something that did not previously exist. Some projects are totally different whist others may contain some elements similar to previous projects. It is the unique elements of projects that make them so challenging and are the major sources of Risk.

- Projects are Finite and Temporary. They have a start point and an end point.

- Projects have defined Deliverables. Whether it is a physical product, a piece of software or a service delivery there will be a specification that defines the characteristics and quality parameters of the end product. An Acceptance Test will take place to determine whether the product meets the specification.

- Projects generally require Teams and teams need Organising and Leading

1.2   Projects v Operations (Business as usual)

'Operations' is the term used to describe the normal business processes and operations conducted by the company or organisation as it undergoes its day to day business. Much of it consists of repeatable and routine management processes. It provides the services and products for business customers on a daily and continuous basis.

It is focused on such things as:-

- Meeting business performance targets such as quality, revenue and profit

- Ensuring that owners, shareholder and the taxpayer get value for money
- Satisfying customer needs and requirements
- Handling issues and problems

Projects and operations have to exist side by side but have very different characteristics. Projects are **Unique** and **Finite** whereas Operations are characteristically **Repetitive** and **Ongoing.** Projects are normally **Revolutionary** in that their outcome is normally a step change in the way something operates. Operations on the other hand are **Evolutionary** in the sense that organisations strive for continuous improvement in small non-disruptive steps.

Because of their uniqueness Projects involve **Risk and Uncertainty.** The performance of Operations is based on cumulative **Experience** that minimises or eliminates risk.
Projects are normally carried out by a **Specially Assembled Team** that only exists for the life of the project. For stability and efficiency Operations requires a **Permanent Workforce** with minimal turnover.

In summary, Projects take place in an environment that is **Dynamic and Changing** whereas the efficiency of an Operation relies on a **Stable and Predictive** environment.

1.3   The Key Purpose of Project Management

Project Management can be briefly described as **"the controlled implementation of a defined change"**

A longer description is provided by BS6079

'Planning, monitoring and control of all aspects of a project and the motivation of all those involved in it to achieve the project objectives, on time and to the specified cost, quality and performance'

Planning, monitoring and controlling are the mechanical aspects of project management. The most difficult aspect of project management is the leading and motivation of the project team, especially when things are not going well. Being good at the mechanical tasks is not sufficient to make a good project manager. Leadership skills are paramount. See later.

1.4   The Core Components of Project Management

- **Planning:**
    - Making sure plans are in place to meet the project objectives

- **Organising/Integrating:**
    - Co-ordination of the mixture of human, financial and physical assets

- **Monitoring**
    - Monitoring progress in relation to time, cost & quality and customer satisfaction

- **Controlling**
  - Taking corrective action when actual performance deviates from the plan

- **Leading/Motivating**
  - Leading and motivating the team and seeing to the needs of individuals

- **Reporting/Communicating**
  - Keeping stakeholders informed of progress and issues

1.5 The Benefits of Project Management

Nowadays organisations accept that in order to introduce change they need the disciplines inherent in formal project management. The major benefits arising from formal project management include:-

- Boundaries and constraints are determined up-front
- The tools and techniques of project management are designed to implement change efficiently.
- A business case has been made and success criteria defined
- The sponsor understands what the deliverables are and how they will be demonstrated, early in the project
- Bring order, structure and discipline to a unique and non-repeatable undertaking
- Reduce the risk of failure from poor investment decision-making, scope creep, inadequate specification, overstated benefits, under-costing etc.
- Monitoring and control processes designed to maximise the chance that deliverables are achieved
- Accountability for the project is centred on one individual, the PM
- Accountability for achieving stated benefits is also centred on one individual, the Sponsor.
- Organisations learn from Post-Project Reviews
- The project organisation is geared to change. It is multi-disciplined with few functional interests.
- Enables sharing of expensive or critical resource across projects

1.6 Programme Management

A Programme is a group of projects that are inter-related and/or interdependent and contribute to a common strategic objective. Although each project is managed independently there must be overall coordination. This is the role of Programme Management.

- Programme Management is a strategic tool. Programmes are generally overseen by the CEO and the Board.

- Projects in a programme can be in parallel or in series or a combination of both. Hence programs can be finite or ongoing

- Projects within a Programme still have individual project managers who report to the programme manager who in turn reports either to a senior sponsor who could be a board member or to the board itself.

1.6.1 Benefits of Programme Management

In a complex organisation it is very easy for individual projects to lose site of overall corporate objectives. A way of avoiding this is to make sure that projects are coordinated via programme management. There are substantial benefits from this approach: e.g

- Programmes will ensure project objectives are in line with corporate objective
- There will be more efficient use of resources because they will be allocated with regard to overall programme requirements rather than individual projects
- Coordination will be carried out all across projects in the programme
- Risks are managed across the programme
- Programme Management provides a strategic tool for managing business projects and keeps the focus on the business change objectives
- Programme Management encompasses the whole Value Chain and avoids point solutions that may be sub-optimal.

1.6.2 Programme Manager Roles & Responsibilities

The principal responsibility of the programme manager is to ensure that the objectives of the programme are met. In order to do this the programme manager:-

- Must ensure that all project managers share a vision across the whole of the programme so that all project plans are fully aligned with the programme objectives.
- Will act as the link between individual projects and project boards and the programme board and must ensure that all information flow both between projects and upwards to the programme board is timely and accurate.
- Must ensure that all projects are progressing in line with the requirements of the programme
- Makes sure that scarce resources are prioritised across projects for maximum programme benefit
- Acts as manager and mentor to the individual project managers

Unless asked for assistance the programme manager does not normally get involved with the detail of individual projects but is responsible for managing the interfaces between them and resolving conflicts between them.

1.7 Portfolio Management

There are two overlapping definitions of what we mean by a portfolio.

a) In a total business context a portfolio is defined as the totality of all an organisation's programmes, projects and related operational activities.

b) A portfolio can also be described as a set of projects or programmes that have no interdependencies and do not share a common objective. Projects may share resources but they are otherwise unconnected. Portfolio management is particularly concerned with the management of resources across competing projects and programmes with particular regard to:-

- Scarce or limited resources and capacity bottleneck

- Balance across the portfolio between risk and return

- Timing of the project i.e. when it takes place

Portfolio managers must ensure that senior management are provided with all the information they require in order to make appropriate decisions regarding the portfolio and will assist and influence them in making those decisions and making sure that the portfolio supports the strategy of the organisation.

1.7.1 Benefits of managing groups of projects as a portfolio

- There is a strategic link between programmes, projects and BAU operations to ensure that all the activities of the organisation are supporting business objectives.

- The same governance principles are applied to all organisational activities.

- Resource allocation considers the requirements of the entire organisation so that an optimum balance can be made between projects and BAU

- Risks and returns can be optimised across the entire portfolio

- There will be a more efficient integration of the output of projects into operations

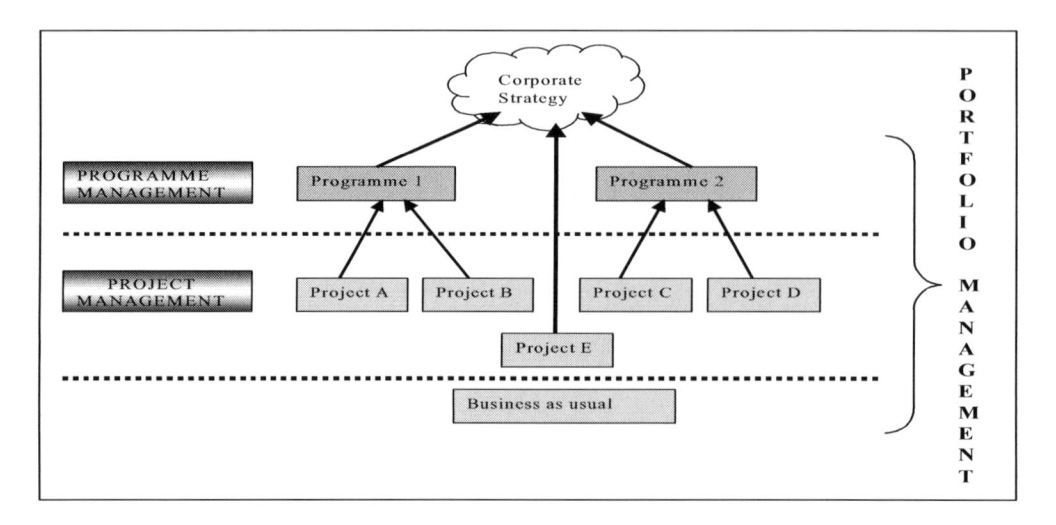

Figure 1.1 Relationship between project, programme and portfolio management

1.7.2 Key Differences Between Programmes and Portfolios

- Projects in a Programme are always inter-related and interdependent whereas projects in a Portfolio can have no dependencies apart from possible resource conflicts.

- Projects in a Programme all contribute to the same defined strategic objective. A portfolio can support several strategic objectives.

- In a Programme all projects must usually succeed for the programme to succeed whereas in a Portfolio failures can be compensated by successes in other projects.

- As all elements of a programme contribute to the same strategic goals the programme manager can switch resources and priorities between projects. This is less true with portfolios.

1.8 The Project Management Triangle

The interaction of Time, Cost and Quality/Performance is usually represented by the Project Management Triangle, sometimes referred to as the triple constraint. In the centre of the triangle lie Health & Safety and Customer Satisfaction. These should be paramount on any project.

It is rare that a project goes exactly to plan. There will be changes, both planned and unplanned and the whole project is subject to risk and uncertainty. When deviations occur one or more of the triple constraints has to give. For example if a project is behind schedule more resources may be needed to catch up. This will increase cost. If the budget is fixed then it may be necessary to reduce quality or functionality. The responsibility for making such decisions lies with the Sponsor and his Board. The job of the project manager is to advise on the possible options and their implications.

Projects take place in a cloud of uncertainty. The Project Manager is constantly maintaining a balance between time, cost and quality with due regard to health and safety and with the constant goal of achieving customer satisfaction.

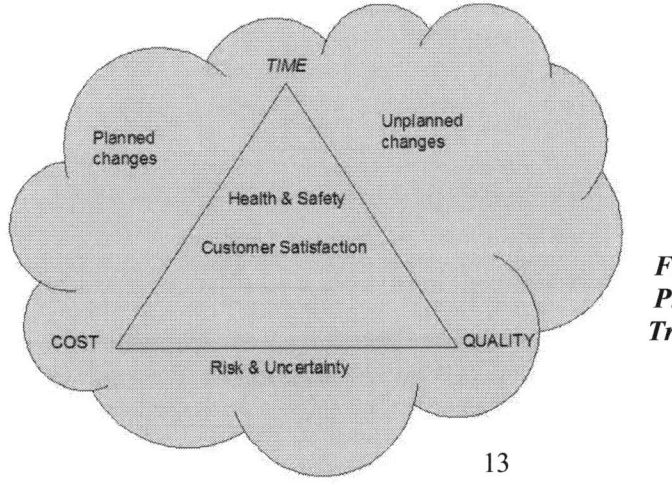

Figure 1.2 Project Management Triangle.

1.9 Project Environment (Context)

Projects do not take place in a vacuum. Each project takes place in its own particular business and technical environment and the successful accomplishment of a project generally requires a significant sensitivity to, and appreciation of, this environment or "context ".

Some of these environmental factors are within the control of the project personnel but many are not. Many of them can significantly affect the project outcome hence they need to be monitored. Generic examples of the kind of things that make up the project context are shown in fig 1.4. These include elements that cover both the internal and external environment of the projects. The project/programme manager and the project sponsor share a responsibility for monitoring the project environment. In general terms the project manager would be primarily concerned with the internal environment and the sponsor with the external environment.

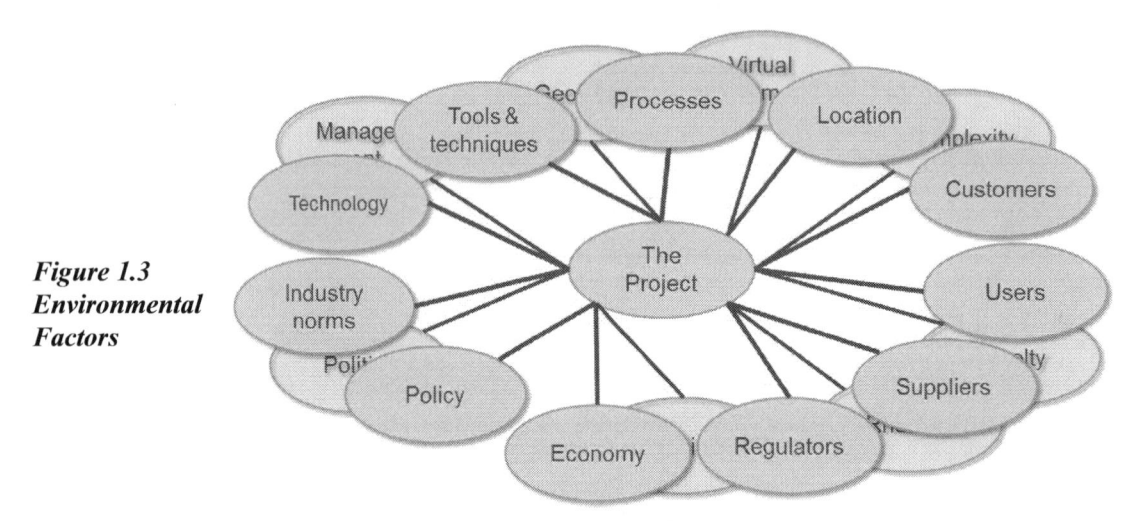

Figure 1.3 Environmental Factors

1.10 Environmental Impact Analysis (EIA)

Investigating the project context is known as Environmental Impact Analysis. An EIA should be carried out as early in the project as possible, typically during the Feasibility stage. The elements identified as being significant will then be continuously monitored. It effectively constitutes part of Risk Management planning.

A common tool that can be used to facilitate an EIA is "PESTLE"

PESTLE is an acronym that stands for:-

- **P**olitical
- **E**conomic
- **S**ociological
- **T**echnological
- **L**egal / Regulatory
- **E**thical/Environmental

PESTLE is simply a tool for providing some structure to the analysis. Possible examples under each of the headings are as follows:-

- Political
  - Taxation
  - Government Policies
- Economic
  - Interest rates
  - Economic outlook
- Social
  - Current Fashions
  - Demographics
- Technology
  - eCommerce
  - Leading edge
- Legal
  - Employment law
  - Environmental regulations
- Ethical
  - Job losses
  - 3rd world exploitation

2 Project Life Cycles and Reviews

Learning Objectives

- Describe the phases of a project that make up a typical project life cycle

- Understand the need for phasing in projects

- Describe the various kinds of project reviews

2.1 A Generic Lifecycle

A project life cycle consists of a sequence of distinct phases or stages. There are many varieties of life cycles which vary across different industries and organisations. Shown below is a generic lifecycle which can be applied to many different kinds of project.

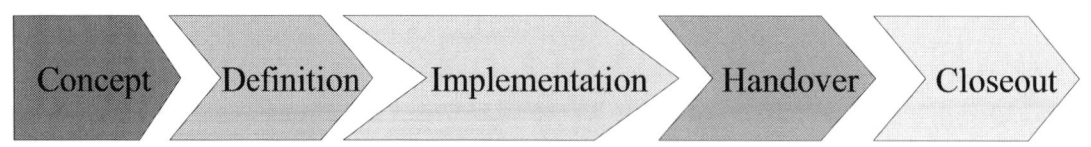

Concept → Definition → Implementation → Handover → Closeout

Figure 2.1 A Generic Lifecycle

In the **Concept** phase the need/problem/opportunity emerges and the proposed solution is tested for technical and financial feasibility. At this stage plans may be at a very low level of details and estimates of costs and timescales are at a low level of accuracy. Plans only need to be accurate enough to decide whether the project is worth continuing into the next phase.

The **Definition** phase is where detailed plans are formulated and if the project is still feasible it will progress to the **Implementation** stage. This stage is often broken down into further sub-phases. Upon completion and acceptance by the client the **Handover** takes place and the **Closeout** phase formally **closes** the project down.

2.2 The Extended Project Life Cycle

In the Extended Project Life Cycle illustrated below, the Operational and Termination phases of the project deliverables are included. This is the life cycle referred to in BS6079 – The British Standard guide to project management. However most authorities refer to this as a **Product** life cycle as projects are considered complete once **Handover** takes place

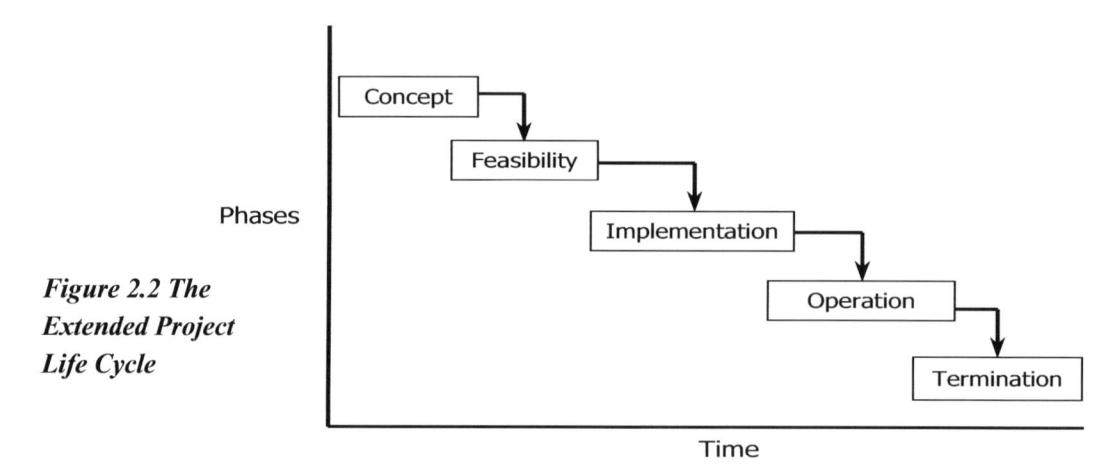

Figure 2.2 The Extended Project Life Cycle

Note that there are no universally accepted names for project phases. **Concept** often includes **Feasibility** and vice versa and the first phase is sometimes called **Initiation.**

Design & Development are sometimes treated as separate phases or often just referred to as the **Planning** phase or the **Definition** phase.

The **Implementation** phase is often called the **Execution** phase.

Closeout is often referred to as the **Exit** phase.

2.3   Benefits of Phasing

The following are some of the benefits that arise from breaking project into phases.

- Identification smaller chunks of work that are more manageable in terms of time, cost and specification
- Provide sponsor/manager checkpoints and gate review points
- Encourage rolling-wave planning*
- Improves the accuracy of estimating
- Focuses on the right work at the right time in the right order
- Application of specialist resource to each phase
- Reduce the risk by committing to a phase at a time
- Phase completion shows evidence of progress

*Rolling-wave planning is where activities taking place in the near future are planned in depth whilst those further out, in later phases, are planned in outline only. Thus as time passes the planning "wave" advances.

2.4   Project Reviews

There are several types of project reviews and there is no consistency in vocabulary between organisations and this can cause confusion.

2.4.1 Phase, Stage or Gate reviews

This review is carried out at the end of each project Phase/Stage*. The boundaries between Phases/Stages are sometimes known as "gateways". At each gateway the project manager must report back to the project board or sponsor and ask for authority to "pass through the gate" i.e. proceed to the next phase. The board will review progress to date against the original baseline plan and any approved changes. They should also revisit the business case

in order to determine if it is still valid. The main benefits of this process are that bad projects can be stopped before too much money has been spent whilst good projects will increase management confidence and commitment.

2.4.2 Project Status reviews

Project Evaluation reviews can be carried out either routinely at set intervals are as a result of a trigger e.g.

- Major milestone reached
- Project crisis
- Major scope changes
- Change of management

The review could cover the whole project or just particular aspects. e.g.

- Technical issues
- Resources
- Governance
- Schedule and budget
- Requirements
- Business case

2.4.3 Project Audits

As mentioned previously, project audits are a component of Quality management. Their purpose is not to look at project progress but to examine if defined processes, policies and procedures are being correctly followed and adhered to. Audits can be internal to the project, within the organisation but outside the projects or from external regulatory bodies.

2.4.4 Post Project Review/Lessons Learned Review

This is a review of the management of the project and is carried out at the end of the project. Prince 2 calls this the Project Evaluation Review. It is covered under Handover & Closeout later in this chapter

2.4.5 Benefits Realisation review/Post Implementation review

This is an evaluation of the project outcome compared to that predicted in the Business Plan. . Prince 2 confusingly calls this the Post Project Review.

2.4.6 Peer Reviews

A Peer review is the evaluation of work by people of similar seniority and competence of the people carrying out the work.

2.5 Handover

Handover consists of all those activities involved with the formal transfer of ownership from the project team to the client/sponsor and end users. It could be a simple handover of product and documentation or a more lengthy process involving testing and training.
The process must demonstrate that the deliverables conform to the specified performance requirements. The handover process must be planned and documented in the project plan.

- Handover must be formal and recorded to ensure transfer over of responsibilities and ownership
- Products/facilities must be subject to pre-agreed acceptance tests
- All pertinent documentation must be signed off
- A process must be in place to handle any outstanding problems e.g snags/bugs
- Terms and conditions of warranties and maintenance must be agreed and documented.

2.5.1 A Handover Process

1. Prepare the Handover Plan. This should be agreed with the Client. It will define all the steps of the handover process, roles and responsibilities and acceptance criteria and any ongoing support and training requirements.

2. Preparation and testing of deliverables by the project team prior to formal handover.
This is to ensure that the handover will go smoothly.

3. Carry out acceptance tests with the Client and users. These tests will be those previously agreed with the client end user representatives.

4. Document results of tests and if satisfactory transfer responsibility and formal ownership. If the tests are not satisfactory the process may have to be stopped whist remedial actions take place.

5. Agree and document outstanding issues regarding bug fixes/snagging lists. Even though the deliverables may pass Acceptance there will probably still be minor outstanding issues

6. Hand over all deliverables and transfer responsibility and formal ownership.

2.6 Closeout

Closeout is concerned with closing the project down in a consistent and organised manner. It should include all the following activities.

- **Tidying up and archiving of project files**
  - All project documentation must be sorted, filed and indexed to facilitate later retrieval to cover issues such as Technical, Financial, Legal, Copyright, IPR etc
- **Financial Accounting**
  - All monies received and paid

- o All costs and revenues reconciled to baseline budget plus changes
- o All surplus stocks and equipment properly disposed of
- **Staff**
  - o Staff demobilised and appropriate feedback given
  - o Recognition of individual and team performance
  - o Appropriate staff retained/obtained to cover warranties and maintenance
- **Closeout meetings**
  - o Formal closeout meetings held with Client and sub-contractors to ensure that all outstanding issues have been addressed
- **Prepare for Post Project Review**

2.7 Post Project Review

The post-project review evaluates the project against its success criteria. Its primary aim is to ensure that lessons learnt can be applied to improve the strategy, planning and management of future projects.

- The post project review occurs after handover of the project deliverables i.e. all work completed and signed off.
- It is the management review at the end of the project and does not consider the technical issues.
- The PM is responsible for ensuring it takes place but should not lead it. This should be done by an independent facilitator
- It should be a non-confrontational meeting. Its purpose is not to allocate blame

2.7.1 Agenda

- History of the project
- Performance of the project organisation
- Accuracy of project planning and estimating Reasons behind variances between plan and actual
- Suitability of monitoring and control systems
- Suitability of the project strategy for the option selected in the investment appraisal

It does not consider benefits realisation. This is the subject of the future Post Implementation Review and is the responsibility of the sponsor.

2.7.2 Planning considerations

Things to consider when planning a Post Project Review

- Who will facilitate it?
- Who should be present?
- Where will it take place?
- When and how long?
- How will the agenda be organised?
- Who will record the conclusions and lessons learned and produce the report?
- How will the lessons learned be disseminated?

3 Roles and responsibilities

Learning Objectives

- Define the responsibilities of the project manager.

- Define the responsibilities of the project sponsor (executive).

- Define the responsibilities of the users.

- Define the responsibilities of the project team members.

- Define the responsibilities of the project steering group (project board)

3.1 The Project Manager

As well as the core activities described in paragraph 1.4 the Project Manager has four key responsibilities within his role..

- **Integrator**
    - Project Integration involves all those activities needed to ensure that people, procedures and work of the project is carried out in a coordinated fashion. The project manager is the only person aware of all the project activities and how they relate to each other.
- **Communicator:**
    - The project manager must ensure that efficient communication channels are set up within the project organisation. A project manager who fails to disseminate information on time can become the major bottleneck in a project.
- **Leader:**
    - Leadership is not the same as management. The project manager must be able to solve problems, guide people from different areas, co-ordinate the project and lead by example.
- **Decision Maker:**
    - The project manager must have the self-confidence to make key decisions even if some risk is involved. A key aspect of project management is knowing when to make a decision and when to consult the sponsor.

3.2 Project Organisation Structure

The figure below shows a typical project structure

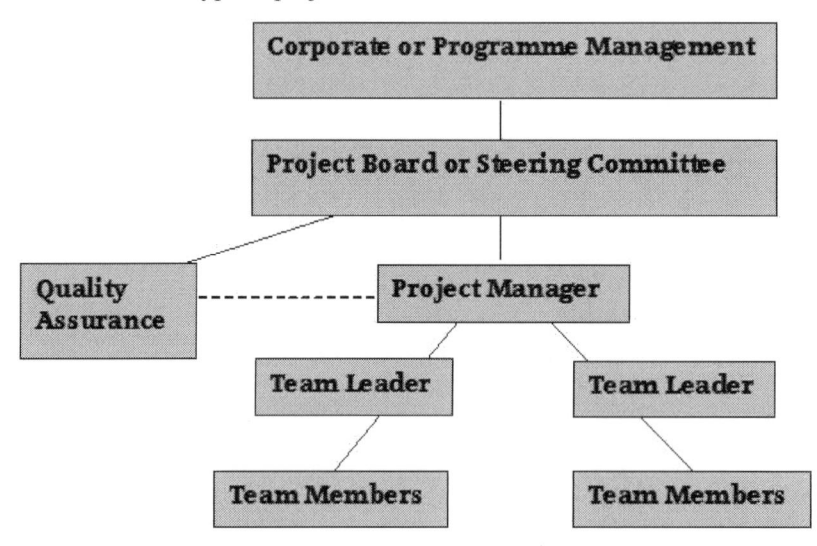

Figure 3.1 Project Structure

3.3 The Project Board

The project board oversees the project from initiation to benefits realisation under the chairmanship of the Project Sponsor. The PM will formally report to the Board at regular intervals and at "Gate" reviews.

A typical make up of a Board is as follows:-

- Project Sponsor (Chair)
- Client (if appropriate)
- End user representative
- Key Suppliers/Sub-contractors
- Appropriate functional managers

3.4 The Project Sponsor

It is vital that a project has an effective sponsor. The sponsor is responsible for justifying the project and arranging project finance and carries overall responsibility for the project from feasibility to benefits realisation. For a successful project there needs to be a continuing dialogue between sponsor and project manager.

The sponsor needs to be:-

- A manager with enough seniority to work across organisational boundaries
- Be an effective Champion of the project and the change it will bring about
- Have enough project management knowledge to judge the effectiveness of the project
- Be supportive of the project manager and have sufficient time to allocate to the role

3.4.1 Sponsor responsibilities

- Chair the Project Board
- Make the business case
- Be the project Champion
- Obtain approval for expenditure
- Make sure business benefits are realised
- Terminate the project if necessary
- Determine the relative priority of Time, Cost & Quality

3.4.2 Sponsor activities

- Define the project's success criteria
- Define the business investment aims
- Initiate the project and ensure a project manager is appointed
- Support the project manager

- Monitor project progress & make control decisions when necessary
- Monitor the project's external environment/context
- Keep senior management informed

3.5 The Project Team & Team Leaders

On all but the smallest projects there will generally be a team leader or leaders to whom the project manager will delegate the necessary authority to execute agreed work packages. The project manager manages the project team members through the team leaders. The team leaders themselves will obviously require project management skills.

It is important that all the team members are aware of, and are committed to the overall project goals so that they can work together towards a common goal and hopefully a shared reward.

3.6 The End Users

The end users are defined as the group of people who are intended to benefit from the project. It is important to realise that they are your ultimate customers and they will be the arbiters of the quality of your deliverables. It is possible to deliver a project on time, to budget and to the specification. However if the end users are not satisfied then the project has failed. To guard against this it is of crucial importance that end user representatives are closely involved in specifying the requirements and in devising acceptance tests for the deliverables. They should be consulted and kept informed throughout the project life cycle.

3.7 Quality Assurance

The Quality Assurance function reports directly to the project board. It is concerned with the correct governance of the project. It has no powers to interfere in the management of the project but will carry out regular Quality Assurance reviews and inform the board as to the outcome.

3.8 The Project Office

All organisations that take project management seriously will have a project office that exists to support the organisation's project needs. Major projects and/or programmes may have their own dedicated support office. Where a project office does not exist the services must be provided from within the project.

At its simplest level the project office may just provide administrative support to project personnel. At the other extreme can become the "Centre of Excellence" for project management and the body to which project managers report. It will be the overseeing body for all project activity and be responsible for linking corporate strategy to project execution.

The presence of a project office allows an organisation to draw together its project management expertise, and makes possible the development of that expertise into a centre of excellence. A project management office fits particularly well with a strong matrix organisation as project managers and project office staff can be brought under common management. However for functional and weak/balanced structures some sort of project office is vital in order to facilitate a common approach to managing projects.

The Project Office can have various names depending on the organisation and the extent of its role e.g.

- PSO -Project Support Office
- PMO-Project Management Office
- EPMO-Enterprise Programme Management Office

3.8.1 Project Support Office-PSO

There are no exact definitions as to what functions each of the above project office types can carry out but as a basic minimum a **Project Support Office** should provide the following functions:-

- General administrative support to project managers and team members
- Collection and treatment of routine project data such as time sheets
- Consolidation of individual project status reports into programme and corporate reports including exception reporting
- Consolidation and dissemination of lessons learned

3.8.2 Project Management Office-PMO

As the PSO takes on more tasks it may be renamed PMO and add functions such as:-

- Project quality audit and assurance
- Identification, development and maintenance of PM methodology, standards, documents, templates etc.
- Co-ordination of resource allocation across all projects
- Selection, operation and management of project tools such as enterprise wide project management software
- Development and management of PM job descriptions and training programmes and professional development.
- Organisation of mentoring and skills development
- Organise and facilitate Gateway Reviews and Post Project Reviews
- Line management of project managers

3.8.3 Enterprise Programme Management Office-EPMO

Ultimately the project office takes on a strategic role within the organisation and becomes the EPMO. It reports directly to a Board member and can take on the following responsibilities.
- The selection, prioritisation and funding of projects and programmes

- Ensuring that individual projects are consistent with programme and corporate goals throughout their life cycle
- Coordination of risk management initiatives across projects and programmes and business as usual
- Ensuring that Benefit reviews take place
- Ultimate responsibility for project governance
- The Centre of Excellence for all project management matters within the organisation

3.8.4 Benefits of a Project Office

- Provides a focal point for project management
- Provides standardisation across projects and adherence to those standards
- Facilitates cross functional projects
- Aligns projects with corporate goals
- Promotes project management skill development
- Coordinates resources across projects
- Takes away routine tasks from project managers
- Facilitates better project selection and control
- Improved communication with senior management
- Better project selection
- Provides better management visibility
- Captures and implements best practice

4 Project Management Planning

Learning Objectives

- Explain the purpose and content of a Business Case

- Explain the purpose, benefits and content of a typical Project Management Plan

- Describe the Authorship and Ownership of the Project Management Plan

- Understand Success Criteria, Success Factors, Key Performance Indicators and how they relate to each other.

- Describe Benefits and the purpose of Benefits Management

- Define Stakeholders and a Stakeholder Management process

- Explain the importance of Stakeholder Management

- Describe the estimating funnel

- Understand typical estimating methods

- Understand project reporting

4.1 Building the Business Case

4.1.1 Business Case Objective & Purpose

The objective in developing a Business Case is to provide a justification for carrying out the project. It must show the expected costs and benefits of the project and how it fits in with the company strategy and contributes to the corporate goals of the organisation. Not all costs and benefits are tangible, i.e. they cannot easily be expressed in purely monetary terms.

In any organisation there are usually many proposed projects that are competing for limited funds. Therefore the purpose of the Business Case is not just to demonstrate why a project is viable in its own right but also why it should be favoured over others.

The Business Case is prepared very early in the project life cycle. As normally no detailed planning has taken place it is often difficult to decide the level of detail in the Business Plan. The answer is that it should contain enough information to enable a decision to be made as to whether to carry on with the project. The decision can always be modified in the light of more detailed planning.

Every project must in some way contribute to the corporate goals of the organisation.

4.1.2 Contents of a Business Case

- Description of Problem/Opportunity and Scope outline
- Other options (including do nothing)
- Principal reason for carrying it out
- Project Deliverables/Objectives
- Fit to the organisation's business strategy
- Emphasis on Time/Cost/Quality
- Outline Schedule and Major Milestones
- Investments Appraisal
- Expected Costs & Benefits-Both tangible and intangible
- High Level Risks and Assumptions
- Success Criteria
- Assumptions
- Stakeholder Analysis
- Impact on Business as Usual

4.1.3 Constructing a Business Case

In order to construct a business case it is necessary to estimate the costs and expected benefits of the project and produce a budget and schedule. This is effectively the first attempt at a project plan and it is carried out by performing the steps shown in fig 4.1 opposite. It is an iterative process which will become more accurate as the project progresses, experience is gained and more knowledge is obtained

The Business Case will make clear the balance between the expected costs and benefits of the project and the level of risk involved. As the project develops and the true costs and risks emerge it should be continuously reviewed to check that the project continues to meet the business objectives. If not there may be a case for termination or scope change.

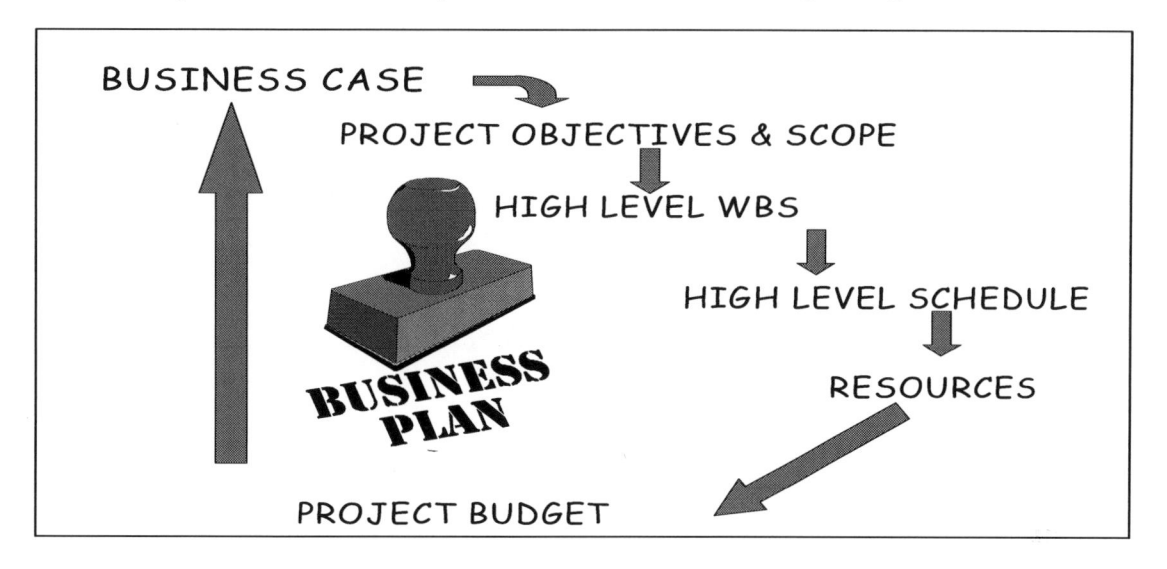

Figure 4.1 Business Plan Construction

4.1.4 Key Contributors to the Business Case

The Sponsor
The Sponsor owns the Business Case and has overall responsibility to the CEO for its production and realisation. This responsibility extends beyond project completion and into operation.

The Project Manager
Ideally the project manager should work with the Sponsor to produce the Business Case and agree the outline budget and schedule and Key Performance Indicators. However in many cases the PM is not appointed at this stage. In that situation the PM should study the business case and discuss any issues with the Sponsor. The PM will also make sure that the project team is aware of the main points of the business case.

Technical Analyst/Consultant
There needs to be an appropriately skilled person who can verify the technical feasibility of the project.

Financial Accountant
Similarly there needs to be someone to verify the financial feasibility.

Client/End user

Where appropriate an end user representative should confirm the objectives and requirements.

4.2 Success and Benefits Management

4.2.1 Project Success Criteria

Defined by APM as:-

"T*he qualitative or quantitative criteria by which the success of a project is judged".*

Possible examples are:-

- Delivered within Time & Budget tolerance
- Delivered to Performance Specification
- Customer Satisfaction rating achieved
- Health & Safety adhered to
- Business Benefits realised
- Increased market share
- Improved productivity

From the point of view of the Project Manager success may be defined as delivering to time, cost and specification. However other stakeholders may be more concerned with business benefits. These will not be known at time of handover. It is perfectly possible for a project to be deemed a delivery success but fail to produce its business benefits. On the other hand many projects delivered late and over budget have nevertheless delivered considerable business benefits.

4.2.2 Project Success Factors

Project Success Factors are those elements within the structure and context of the project that are conducive to success. Their presence will not guarantee success but their absence will markedly increase the probability of failure.

Examples are:-
- Clear project mission
- Top management support
- Client consultation
- Committed project personnel
- Monitoring and feedback mechanisms
- Clear communications
- Adequate resources

4.2.3 Key Performance Indicators

Key Performance Indicators are continuously measured over the life of the project. They directly measure the project performance against Project Success Criteria. Although success criteria can be qualitative or quantitative ideally they should be SMART. i.e.

Specific **M**easurable **A**ccountable **R**ealistic **T**imely

4.2.4 Project Failure

Very few projects can claim to have met all of their success criteria and hence, at least technically, can be said to have failed. There are many reasons why projects fail. Following are some of the more common reasons:-

- Lack of end user involvement
- Poor requirements definition
- Insufficient planning
- Lack of Risk planning and management
- Poor monitoring & Control
- Poor delegation
- High staff turnover
- Lack of sponsorship
- Poor estimating
- Poor change control
- Wrong technology
- Poor development environment
- Lack of control of 3rd parties
- Poor project management

All of these reasons can be reversed to generate success factors.

4.3 Stakeholder Management

A Stakeholder is defined as any person or body that has an interest in a project or its outcome or is affected by it. Stakeholder Management involves the processes of identifying stakeholders, analysing their interest and formulating plans to control or influence them.

The attitude and actions of Stakeholders can have a significant effect on the performance and outcome of your project and hence they must be proactively managed. The influence of stakeholders must be considered right at the start of the project when preparing the business case.

4.3.1 Typical Stakeholders

- Resources needed for the project
- People and Organisations who may be affected by the project

- People and Organisations not directly affected but who may have strong opinions about the project, either positive or negative
- Statutory and regulatory bodies
- Potential end users of the project products

End users are important stakeholders and their requirements must be captured early on when considering project requirements. It is also particularly important to recognise and manage negative stakeholders as if left unmanaged they can have a detrimental effect on the project. The above list is not exhaustive. Each project will have its own particular set of stakeholders.

4.3.2 The Stakeholder Management Process

Figure 4.2 Stakeholder Management Process.

Step1 Identification

The most usual method of identification is by *Brainstorming*. Potential stakeholders may include:
- People affected by the project
- People on the sidelines who may have strong feelings about the project; both positive and negative.
- Statutory and regulatory bodies
- Resource requirements

Relationships between stakeholders can be represented by a Stakeholder Map such as the example shown below which relates to an IT project in a manufacturing environment.

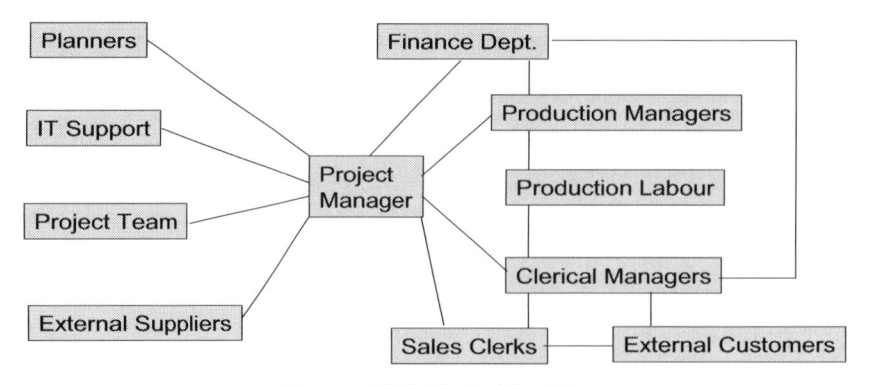

Figure 4.3 Stakeholder Map

Step 2 Analysis

In the analysis stage it is necessary to try and discover the position of stakeholders with respect to the project. Consideration might be given to questions such as the following:

- Will they benefit from the success of the project?
- Will they be openly supportive of the project?
- Do they have reasons for wanting the project to fail?
- If their views are negative or ambivalent can they be persuaded to change?
- What is their level of power and influence?

Information can be summarized using the model shown below in figure 4.4

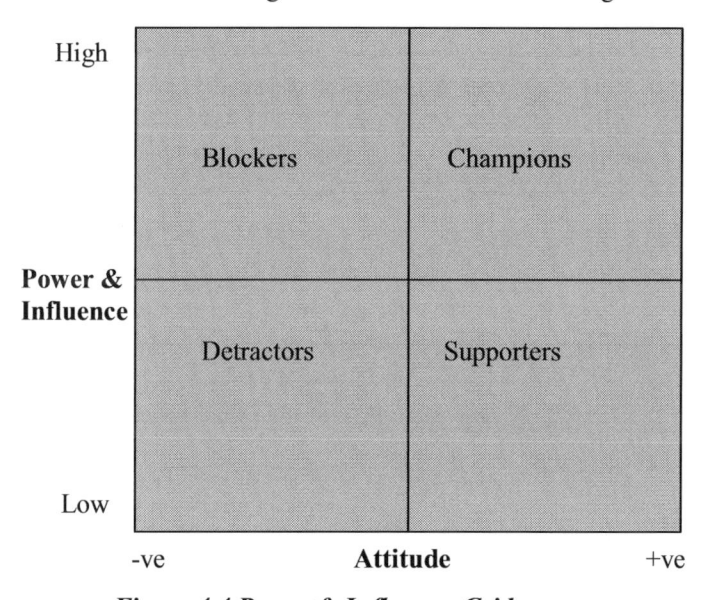

Figure 4.4 Power & Influence Grid

- **Champions** are powerful people who are actively supportive of the project.
- **Blockers** are powerful people who will actively resist the project.
- **Supporters** are people with little power who are in favour of the project.
- **Detractors** are people with little power who are against the project.

Bear in mind that Detractors and Supporters can organise themselves into focus groups and become Blockers and Champions respectively.

Step 3 Planning

Planning consists of examining each stakeholder, trying to understand what is their likely attitude to the project, what motivates them what power they exert and then formulating an action strategy to manage and influence them. A brief example based on the project of figure 4.3 is shown in fig 4.5.

Stakeholder	Attitude	Motivation	Actions
Production Manager	Champion	Success will increase productivity	Regular communication
Production Operatives	Blockers	Possible job losses	Negotiate severance pay and productivity bonus
Sales Clerks	Detractors	Think it will make their job harder	Involve in requirements and acceptance
IT Maintenance	Supporters	New system easier to maintain	Keep onside by regular updates & consultation

Figure 4.5 Stakeholder Action Plan

Step 4 Managing

Stakeholders must be actively managed, especially as their views and motivation may change over the life of the project. The analysis must be repeated throughout the project lifecycle as new stakeholders appear and attitudes change. "Champions" can be used to managing or influencing "Blockers" or to organise "Supporters".
Another key management tool for managing stakeholders is the Communications Plan. This is covered in Chap 9.

4.3.3 Benefits of Stakeholder Management

- Helps identify project risks and opportunities
- Facilitates pro-active mode of operation
- Facilitates managing stakeholder expectations
- Facilitates better working relationships
- Increases confidence of Stakeholders in the Project Manager
- Increases likelihood of project success

4.4 The Project Management Plan

The Project Management Plan documents the planning outcomes of the project and provides the reference point for managing the project. It is the primary document that communicates the project manager's intentions to the Stakeholders. It is owned by the Project Manager and approved by the Sponsor. Although the project manager is responsible for its production it has to be a team activity. As well as ensuring a more robust and accurate plan it also fosters team commitment. It is also the primary tool for Stakeholder communication.

4.4.1 The seven fundamental questions

1) **The "Why"**

    This is developed in the Business Case. It describes the need or problem being addressed and why it is necessary to do so.

2) **The "What"**

> This describes the scope of the project in terms of what exactly what is to be delivered. It will also describe the success criteria and the key performance indicators.

3) **The "How"**

> This describes the project strategy including the tools and techniques to be used, the monitoring and controlling processes and reporting arrangements. It will also cover fundamental decisions such as choice of methodology, life cycle and use of third parties.

4) **The "Who"**

> This describes project roles and responsibilities, organisational structures and plans for human resource acquisition.

5) **The "When"**

> This documents the project schedule including key milestones.

6) **The "Where"**

> This describes the geographical locations where the work will be carried out

7) **The "How Much"**

> This states the project budget with expected spending by time period and by phase.

The Project Management Plan is a live, configuration controlled document which builds upon the information contained in the Business Plan. It provides a contract between the Sponsor and the Project Manager. It is a reference point for reviews, audits and control. It also assists effective handover in the event of a change in project management or sponsorship.

4.4.2 Project Plan Content

As well as the items described above the PMP will document policies and procedures for managing aspects of the project. i.e.

- Quality Management Plan
- Change Management Plan
- Risk Management Plan
- Communications Management Plan
- Procurement Management Plan
- Health & Safety Plan
- Stakeholder Management Plan
- Environmental Impact Analysis

All of these are addressed in other sections of this document.

The Project Management Plan is unlikely to exist as a single hardcopy document. In order to be effectively maintained and be accessible to team members and appropriate stakeholders it is better to have an electronic document that is made available on the organisation's intranet.

4.5 Benefits of Planning

The following are the key benefits that derive from having a well thought out plan:-

- Careful consideration of project scope avoids missing things out
- Problems are anticipated and management is proactive rather than reactive
- Improves understanding - clarifies the real issues
- Concentrates attention on the deliverables
- Provides a basis for monitoring and control of budget and schedule
- Builds commitment in the team through involvement
- Improves confidence and morale of the team and stakeholders
- Establishes achievable targets and milestones
- Identifies resources required
- Establishes responsibilities
- Dramatically increases the probability of a successful project

4.6 Ownership, Authorship and Audience

Ownership

- The PM owns the responsibility for creating and maintaining the plan
- The Sponsor approves the plan and has ultimate responsibility for it
- To be motivated the Project Team must feel ownership and involvement
- Major Stakeholders must also "buy in" to the plan

Authorship

- The PM is the overall author of the PMP. However some subsections may be written by specialist team members e.g. Quality Plan, Procurement Plan

Audience

- The PMP is intended to be read by any legitimate stakeholder. e.g. Sponsor and Board, Team members, Major suppliers, End Users

4.7 Benefits Management

4.7.1 Responsibility

Benefits Management consists of defining the expected business benefits of a project and then monitoring the situation to ensure those benefits are delivered. The benefits of a project are rarely realised at handover and it can take weeks or months before some benefits appear. e.g productivity gains. Although on some occasions the project manager may maintain some involvement it is generally the Sponsor who has prime responsibility for delivering business benefits.

4.7.2 Benefits review

The benefits review typically takes place 6-12 months after handover or when the "solution" has bedded in. The review will be chaired by the Project Sponsor. The people present will be mainly operational although appropriate project personnel may be present.

The review considers all the forecasted benefits of the project as defined in the Business Case and compares them with the outcome. If the benefits are not forthcoming then the reasons are determined and an action plan formulated. Further benefits reviews may be necessary.

4.8 Estimating Methods

An estimate is a quantified assessment of the resources required to complete part or all of the project. It is stated in terms of cost & time & resources. Inaccurate (usually over optimistic) estimating is a major cause of project failure. Some would say it is **the** major cause. Estimates must initially be made at Business Plan stage. These estimates are usually based on high level data but people are often very reluctant to revise them even when experience is showing that they are wrong. It is essential in any project for outcomes to be compared to initial estimates and estimates adjusted if necessary, even if these causes the business plan to be re-examined.

There are three main estimating methods

1. Bottom Up Estimating
2. Comparative Estimating
3. Parametric Estimating

These methods can be used independently but more usually in combination.

4.8.1 Analytical (Bottom Up) Estimating

This method is based on the WBS. All the individual lower level tasks in the WBS are estimated independently and then rolled up to produce the project estimates. This is a laborious method and its accuracy is dependant on having a correct WBS. However it is the most accurate way of estimating. It is sometimes known as the definitive estimate. The aimed for accuracy is to be within 5%.

4.8.2 Comparative Estimating

This is also called Top Down or Historic estimating. It simply involves using experience from similar projects carried out in the past. It takes the overall costs and timescales for similar projects and adjusts them for size and complexity. The danger is that previous projects may have been inefficient and/or badly managed. Comparative estimating can also be used at task level to support bottom up.

4.8.3 Parametric Estimating

Parametric estimating uses a mathematical model or formulae to produce project estimates based on input parameters. It is usually based on historical data. Simple examples are square metres in construction and lines of code in software development. Quantity Surveyors make extensive use of parametric estimating. More complex software applications such as COCOMO and Function Point Analysis are beyond the scope of this book.

4.8.4 The Estimating Funnel

Estimates cost time and money to produce and the more accuracy required the more expense involved. The estimating process typically goes through 5 stages where each estimate is used to justify the effort of producing the next one. The stages are:

	% Accuracy
1. Proposal	-30 to +50
2. Budget	-20 to +35
3. Sanction	-10 to +25
4. Control	-5 to +15
5. Tender	-2 to + 5

We recognise the inaccuracies in the early stages of estimating by applying appropriate contingency allowances. As the project develops and additional information is obtained the accuracy improves and contingencies can be reduced.

The way in which accuracy improves over the project lifecycle can be seen in the "Estimating Funnel" illustrated below.

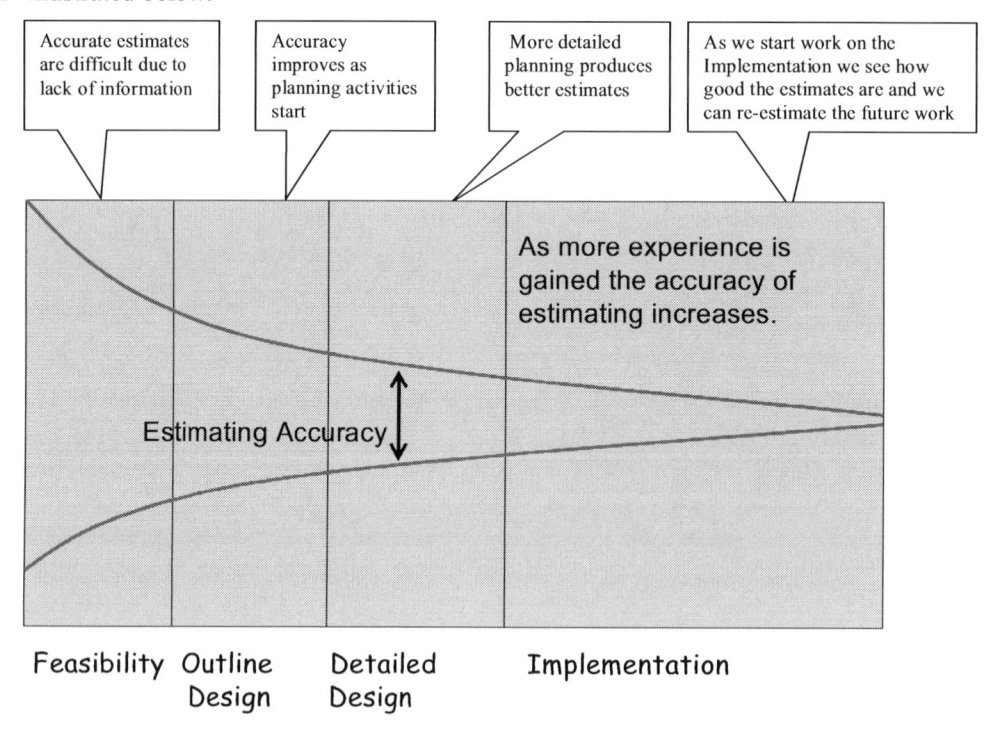

Figure 4.6 The Estimating Funnel

4.9 Project Reporting

It is the responsibility of the PM to ensure that all relevant project information is communicated to the Sponsor and appropriate stakeholders in a timely and effective manner. The benefit of such a process is that by keeping relevant stakeholders informed as to project progress it will avoid misunderstandings and manage expectations. It is a vital part of stakeholder management.

There will be ongoing informal communication at all times but project status should be formally reported, usually on a monthly basis and at key points such as phase ends. To do this the PM will require formal reports from appropriate team members which must then be collated and simplified for passage upwards.

It should be stressed that formal reporting is not a substitute for ongoing project communication. Information must be presented in a timely fashion and it may not be appropriate to wait until the next monthly report. Avoid overloading Stakeholders with too much information and use Exception Reporting when appropriate.

4.9.1 Report Structure

A project status report should be clear and concise with a consistent structure and layout such as the following.

1. A short management summary containing key information. Some stakeholders will not read beyond this.
2. List achievements and progress since last status update was given
3. List delays and problems since last status update was given
   - List corrective actions being taken
   - Address schedule implications
4. Outline Plan for next period
   - Planned deliverables
   - Milestones
   - Potential problems
   - Help required
5. Earned Value Report
   - Earned Value Graph
   - Cost & Schedule Variances
   - Cost & Schedule Completion Forecasts

Note that a study of Earned Value Management is not included in the syllabus. In simple terms Earned Value is a technique for measuring project performance and progress. EVM has the ability to combine measurements of scope, schedule, and cost in a single integrated system. It measures not just cost of work done, but relates this cost to the amount of useful work done with regard to the planned budget and schedule. For a more detailed description see "An APMP Primer" by Robin Kay.

5 Scope Management

Learning Objectives

- Define project scope and scope management

- Describe how work and product breakdown structures are used to define project scope

- Describe
    - Cost Breakdown Structure
    - Organisational Breakdown Structure

- Describe the purpose and use of the Responsibility Assignment Matrix

- Describe a typical Change Control process

- Understand Configuration Management

- Understand the relationship between Change Control and Configuration Management and how they contribute to Scope Management

5.1 Definition of Scope

Scope Management is concerned with all the tools and processes that ensure that enough work, but no more, is carried out to produce the project deliverables. It is concerned with controlling the boundaries of the project and ensuring that all work done is related to project objectives and that any new work is subject to a formal change control process. It is also important to clearly establish what is excluded from the project scope.

The Business Plan will define the breadth of the project scope. As the project progresses the depth of the scope will increase. Scope creep and uncontrolled change are common causes of project failure so if changes are made to the scope breadth then this must be done through a formal change control process.

The primary tools for defining and controlling project scope are the Work Breakdown Structure (WBS) and the Product Breakdown Structure (PBS)

5.2 Work Breakdown Structure

The WBS is an activity based decomposition of the work to be carried out. The project is broken down level by level. The lowest levels are called work packages or tasks depending on the methodology used. Each task/work package (apart from management products) has a defined end product with an associated acceptance test to determine when it is complete. As the WBS contains all the work of the project required to produce the project deliverables it totally defines the project scope.

The WBS is the framework on which the project is built. It is not possible to build a realistic project plan without first developing a WBS that details all the project tasks that must be accomplished. The process of creating the WBS causes the project manager and all involved with the planning process to carefully consider all aspects of the project.

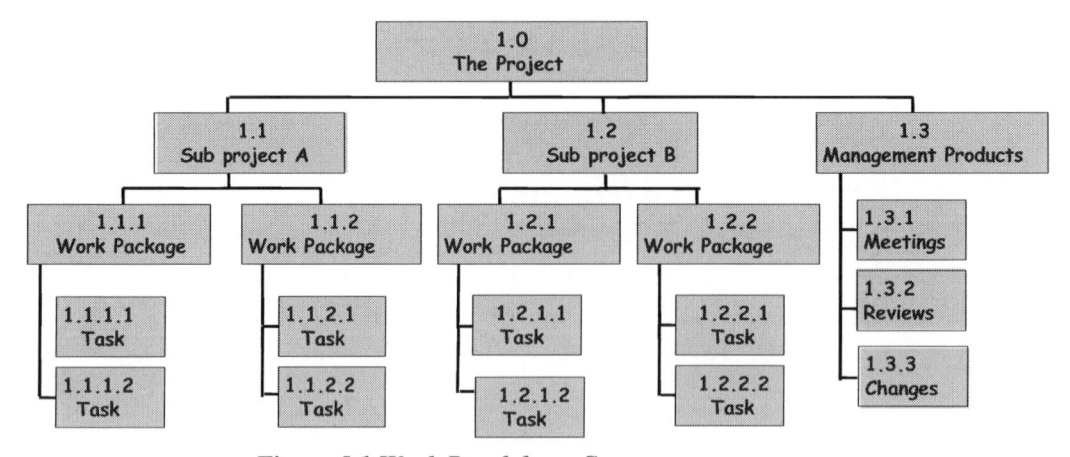

Figure 5.1 Work Breakdown Structure

The WBS shows how each work package contributes to the overall project objectives and so provides a firm basis for both planning and controlling the project. Each work package or task represents the level at which the project manager exerts control. Each WP/task is a self-contained piece of work that can be given to a single person or a small team. Each will have a list of defines attributes:-

- Specification
- Acceptance criteria
- Responsibility
- Budget
- Duration
- Resource requirements
- Dependencies

The size of these Work Packages is very important because they must be small enough to allow realistic estimates to be made, but also not so small that the sheer number of tasks overwhelms the planning and control process.

5.2.1 Benefits of the WBS
- Its production facilitates team building
- It focuses attention on project objectives
- It forces detailed planning
- It facilitates the allocation of responsibility for individual packets of work
- It graphically illustrates project scope
- It is the starting point for:
  o Budgeting
  o Estimating
  o Scheduling
  o Controlling
  o Change Control
  o Configuration Management

5.3 The Product Breakdown Structure

Whereas the WBS is activity related the PBS is product related. It breaks the project down into its constituent products and sub products as illustrated on the next page.

Production of the PBS has 3 main objectives:-

- To identify customer products
- To identify additional products which will facilitate building and supporting these products
- To gain consensus on sensible product grouping

The topmost product is the "final" product or project outcome. The PBS includes as lower level items, products supplied by external sources. Each higher level product is completely defined by the levels below. The PBS will generally include "intermediate" or "enabling" products or "sub-assemblies"

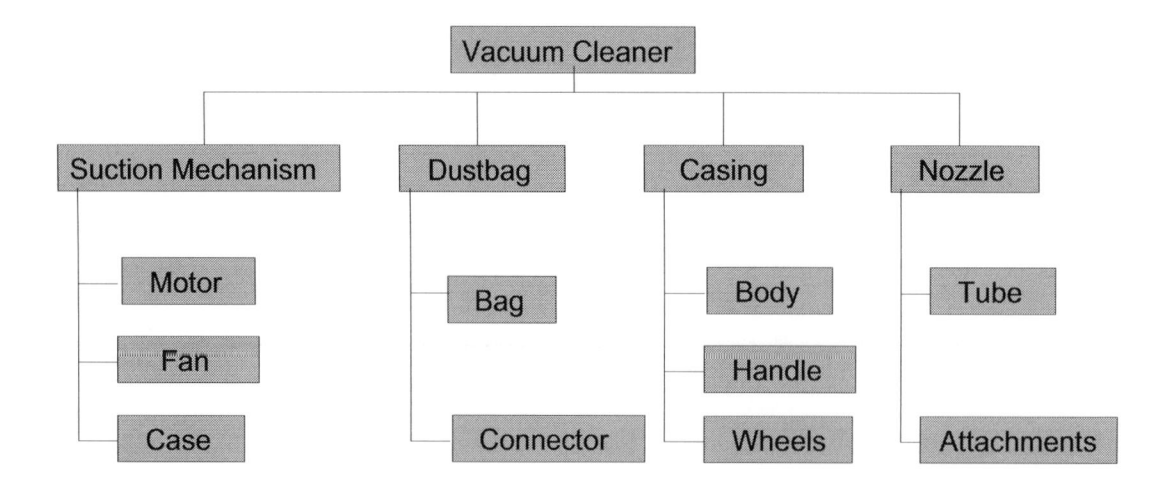

Figure 5.2 Product Breakdown Structure

5.4 Relationship between WBS and PBS

The WBS breaks down the work into individual tasks and each task delivers a "product". The PBS breaks down the product into individual components and each component requires "work". Hence the WBS and PBS are just opposite sides of the same coin; the same solution from a different viewpoint. It is also common to have hybrid situations where a product is broken down into the work needed to produce it. An example is shown below.

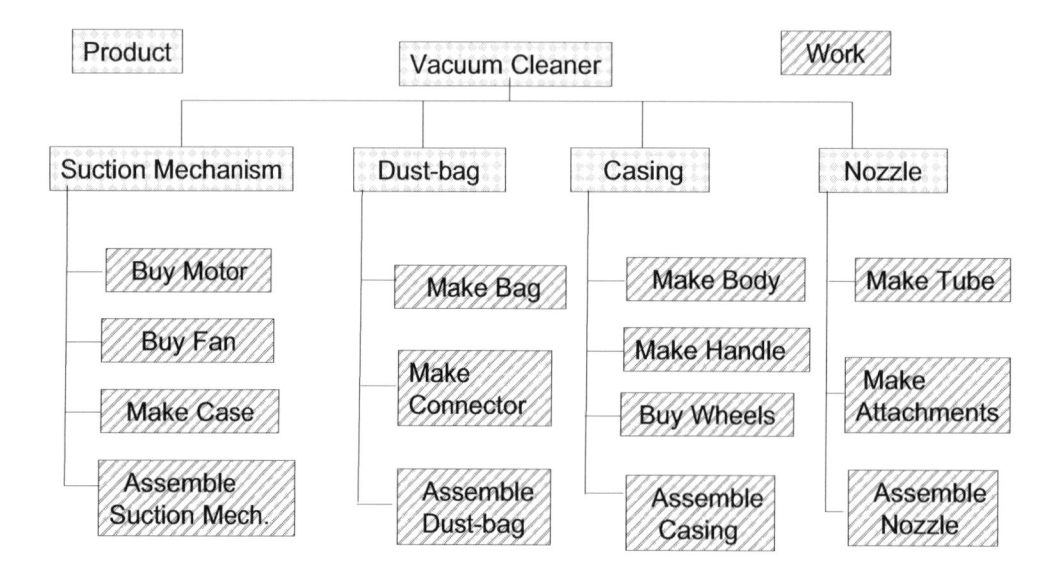

Figure 5.3 Hybrid PBS/WBS

5.5 Cost Breakdown Structure

A CBS shows all the different cost categories that make up the total project costs. The costs are applied to every work package/task on the WBS or end items on the PBS enabling costs to be rolled up to any required level. An example is shown below.

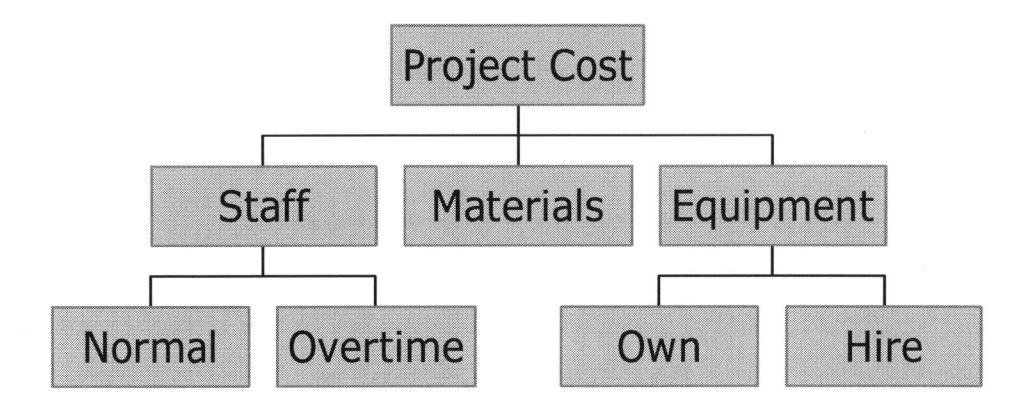

Figure 5.4 Cost Breakdown Structure

5.6 Organisational Breakdown Structure (OBS)

The OBS shows how the project team is organised. A simple example is shown below but more complicated structure can be developed to show how the project team structure relates to the structure of the organisation and communication and reporting lines.

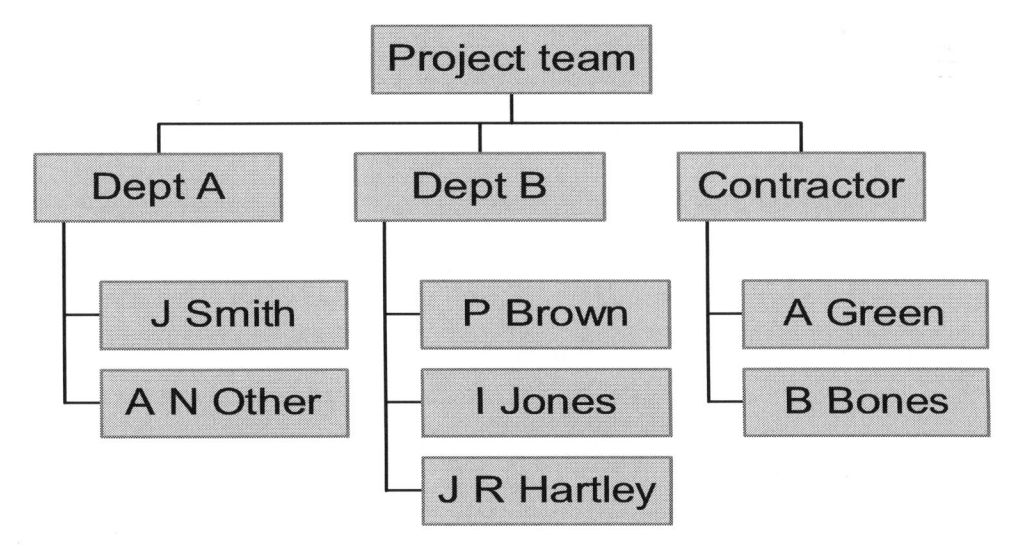

Figure 5.5 Organisational Breakdown Structure

5.7 Responsibility Assignment Matrix (RAM)

The WBS and OBS can be combined to produce the Responsibility Assignment Matrix which shows the personnel required to execute each work package/task.

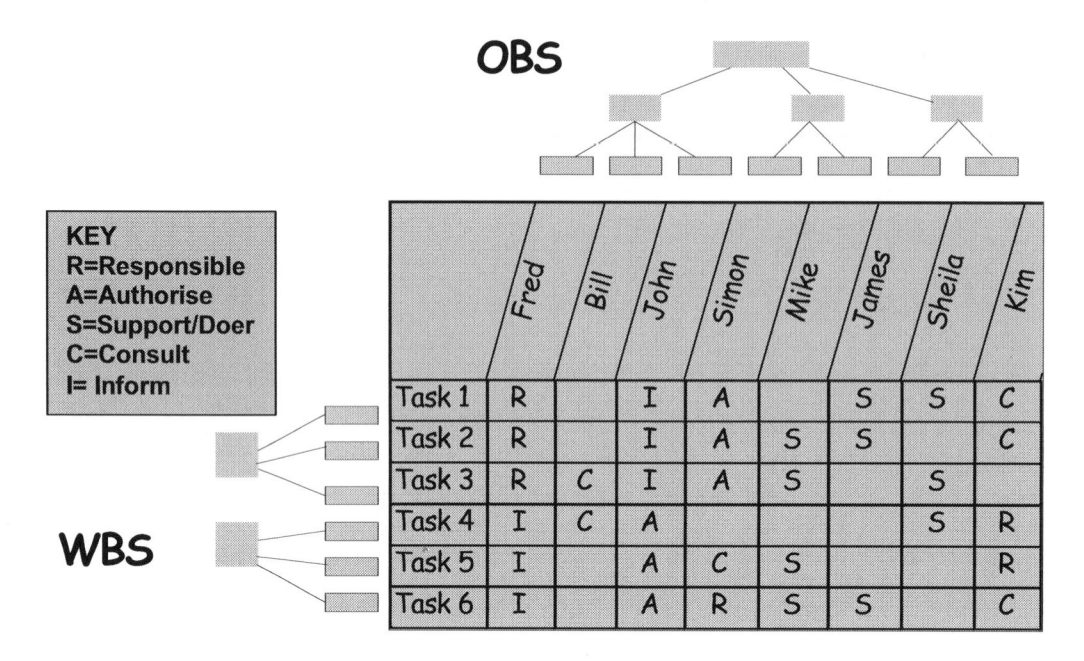

KEY
R=Responsible
A=Authorise
S=Support/Doer
C=Consult
I= Inform

	Fred	Bill	John	Simon	Mike	James	Sheila	Kim
Task 1	R		I	A		S	S	C
Task 2	R		I	A	S	S		C
Task 3	R	C	I	A	S		S	
Task 4	I	C	A				S	R
Task 5	I		A	C	S			R
Task 6	I		A	R	S	S		C

Figure 5.6 Responsibility Assignment Matrix

This is sometimes referred to as a RASCI chart.

5.8 Change Control

5.8.1 Definition of a Change

In a projects context a change is defined as when an event occurs that requires or causes a change to be made to the Project Baseline Plan in terms of scope, cost, time or quality.

Change Control is the process by which all changes are identified and evaluated and then a decision made on whether they are approved, rejected or deferred.
Changes can arise from 3 main areas:-

- From errors, omissions in the original planning.
- From evolution of project requirements or new techniques
- Legal/mandatory changes

Changes are sometimes referred to as Variations

5.8.2 Why Change Control is Important

"Scope Creep", where project scope keeps increasing over time; and uncontrolled change are major causes of project failure. Changes to the project baseline must be evaluated and planned with the same thoroughness as the original plan.

Scope Creep can:-
- Increase project cost
- Cause delays
- Be detrimental to quality
- Reduce morale and productivity

However we cannot prohibit project change, because change is usually beneficial, and in fact many projects would fail if no changes were allowed. In certain circumstances a change freeze may be appropriate but when changes are allowed they MUST be controlled.

Excessive change requests are usually a symptom of poor planning and requirements definition. Proper planning and consultation with all appropriate stakeholders will help minimise change requests.

5.8.3 The Change Control Process

1. The request is entered into the change control system. Change requests must be made in writing in the appropriate standard form.
2. An Owner is assigned to manage the change control process. (Not the change itself)
3. A brief preliminary evaluation is carried to see if it is worth further investigation and to prioritise it.
4. If the answer to the above is yes then an impact analysis is carried out.
5. CCB* Approve, reject or postpone the change request
6. If approved, plans, documentation, timescale and budgets are updated.
7. The Change Log is updated
8. All who are impacted are advised of the changes.

*Note:- CCB means Change Control Board. This is the ideal scenario but when a formal CCB does not exist, decisions will be made by the Client/Sponsor or appropriate Stakeholders or by the PM. Responsibility for minor changes may be delegated but must still go through the same formal process.

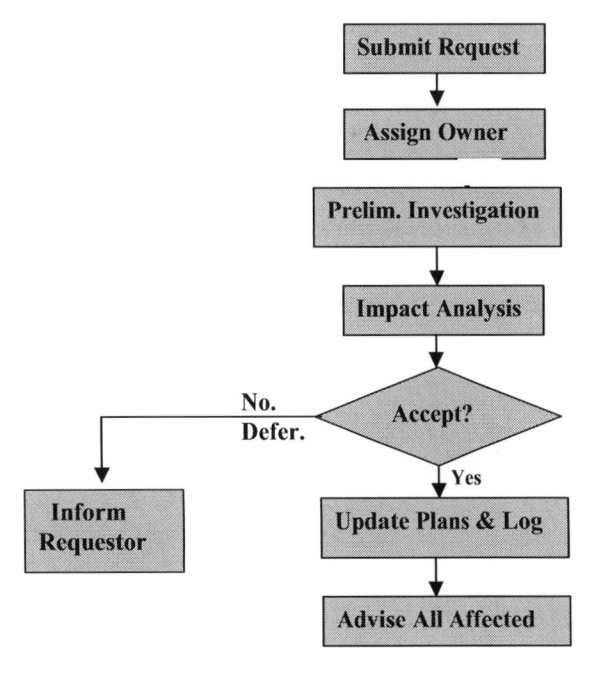

Figure 5.7 Change Control Process

All changes must be authorised so if unauthorised changes are discovered they must be retrospectively be put through the change control process. This may mean undoing some changes.

5.8.4 The Change Request Form

Changes must be formally requested on the appropriate form. Typical contents of a form are shown in the figure below.

PROJECT:	Number Revision Requestor Date
ITEMS AFFECTED	Work Package Nos.
DESCRIPTION OF CHANGE	
REASON FOR CHANGE	
COST & SCHEDULE IMPACT	
EFFECT ON BUSINES CASE	
CONSQUENCE OF NOT DOING CHANGE	
ANY OTHER COMMENTS	
CHANGE APPROVED/REJECTED/REFERRED BACK	
SIGNATURES DATE	

Figure 5.8 Change request Form

5.8.5 Impact Assessment

Impact assessment must be carried out by people who are competent to fully understand the implications of the change on the current baseline plan. They must determine:-

- What would have to change?
- What effort would the change need?
- What is the affect on schedule / budget?
- What are the knock on effects?
- Would the business case alter?
- Would the risks increase or decrease?
- Would the agreed time for delivery change?
- Is the change within agreed tolerances?

Note: That for proposed major changes, the effort involved in analysing the impact can itself have a significant impact on the project and therefore the analysis may need to be formally approved.

5.8.6 The Change Control Log

The Change Control Log consists of the original Change Request form plus a statement of the current status and the ultimate outcome in terms of effect on schedule and budget and any other knock on effects.

The Change Control Log is an important part of the project audit trail. The Baseline Project Plan plus the Change Control Log represent the current state of the project.

Changes to the project will often result in changes to the project configuration so change control is intrinsically linked to configuration management.

5.9 *Configuration Management*

A product, whether it is a physical thing such as a motor car or something ethereal such as software, is made up of many inter-related components. These include documents such as specifications, designs and plans as well as deliverable components. The totality of items is known as the Configuration. Configuration Management encompasses all the activities concerned with the creation, maintenance and change control of the configuration.

As a product is developed it will undergo additions and changes. Changes to one configuration item may impact others. We therefore need to control and manage these knock on effects. Controlling the configuration during the project will ensure the traceability and integrity of the delivered product or products.

The Configuration Management System must be totally aligned with the Change Control System. Its ability to identify possible knock on effects will facilitate change assessment and will also protect different versions of the deliverable.
Configuration Management is not just a project tool but is a key tool in the subsequent operation and maintenance of the project deliverables.

5.9.1 Configuration Management Activities
The configuration management process consists of 5 principal activities:-

1. **Configuration Management Planning**
   Establishes project specific procedures and defines tools, roles and responsibilities
2. **Configuration Identification**
   Breaking down the project deliverables into individual configuration items and creating a unique numbering system.
3. **Configuration Control**
   Maintains version control of all configuration items and the interrelationship between items.
4. **Configuration Status Accounting**
   Recording of all events that have happened to a system under development to allow comparison with the development plan and to provide traceability.
5. **Configuration Audit**
   Carried out to demonstrate that the products produced conform to the current specification and all procedures have been followed

5.9.2 Components of the Configuration Management System

The configuration management system is supported by 4 key sets of documents:-

1. **The Configuration Item Record**
   Where the item is kept, current status, dependencies on other items, cross reference to other information, change history.
   (All configuration items are subject to version control)

2. **The Product Description**
   A comprehensive product specification

3. **The Configuration Status Account**
   History of all changes and additions to the configuration

4. Configuration Audit Records
   Records of all audits carried out.

5.9.3 Link to change control

The Configuration Management System must be totally aligned with the Change Control System. Its ability to identify possible knock on effects will facilitate change assessment and will also protect different versions of the deliverable. The following diagram shows the change control process and its interaction with configuration management.

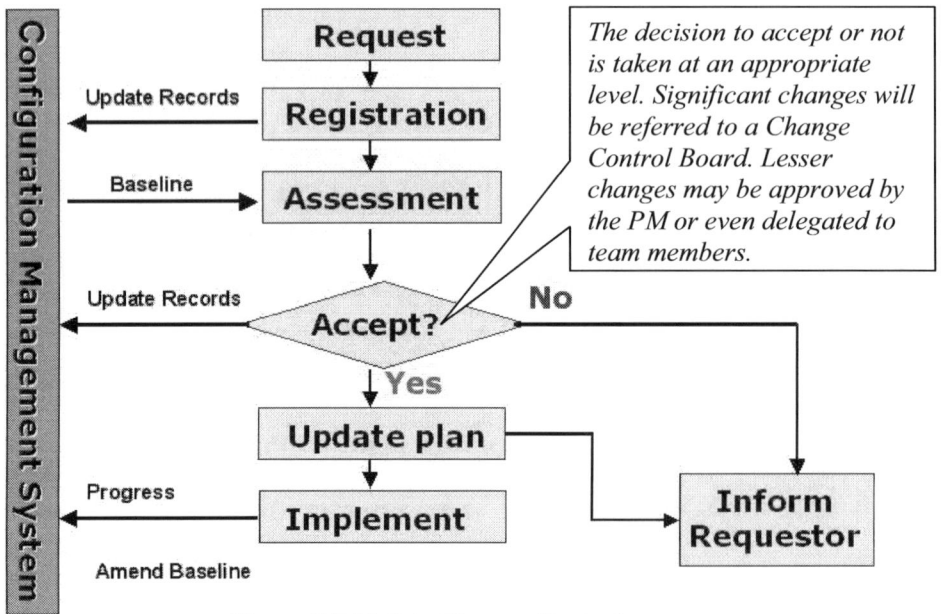

Figure 5.9 Link to Change Control

52

6 Scheduling & Resource Management

Learning Objectives

- Explain the purpose of a schedule and how a schedule is created and maintained

- Understand the following concepts:-

    - Precedence diagrams
    - Critical path
    - Total float and free float
    - Gantt charts
    - Milestone planning
    - Baselines

- Understand resource management and its purpose

- Understand different resource types

- Understand resource smoothing (time limited scheduling)

- Understand resource levelling (resource limited scheduling)

- Understand the process for Resource Procurement

6.1 The Precedence Diagramming Method

There are two distinct methods by which activities can be scheduled. Historically the first method was called the "Activity on Arrow" method where each task to be scheduled is represented by an arrow and the arrows are logically linked to form a network. This method has now been largely superseded by the "Activity on Node" or "Precedence Diagramming Method" (PDM) which is the one used by the vast majority of software packages.

In the Precedence Diagramming Method tasks are represented by boxes with dependencies shown as logical connections between the boxes. A simple example is shown below.

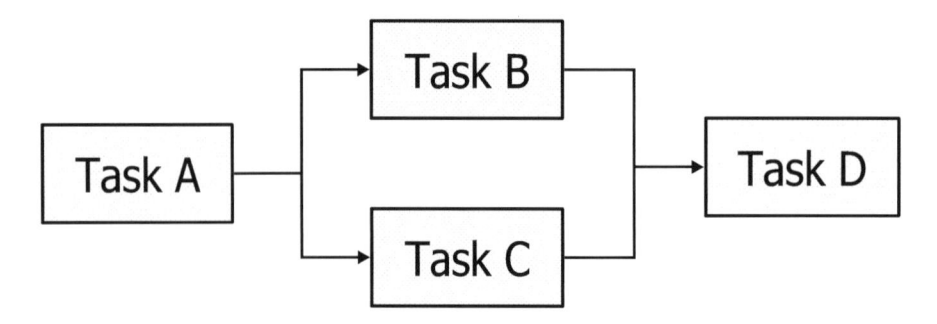

Upon completion of Task A we can start Tasks B and C. Once both these are completed we can start task D. Thus B and C are preceded by A and D is preceded by B and C.

The tasks are derived from the WBS. Each box represents a lowest level task or work package.

6.1.1 Other Link Types & Leads and Lags

The relationship described above (finish to start) is the one most commonly used but there are three other possible relationships making four in all.

1. Start to Start
B can start 2 days after A starts

2. Finish to Finish
D can not finish until 3 days after C finishes

3. Start to Finish
F cannot finish until at least 4 days after E starts

4. Finish to Start
There is at least 1 day between G finishing and H starting.

Leads and lags
Leads originate from start times and lags from finish times.

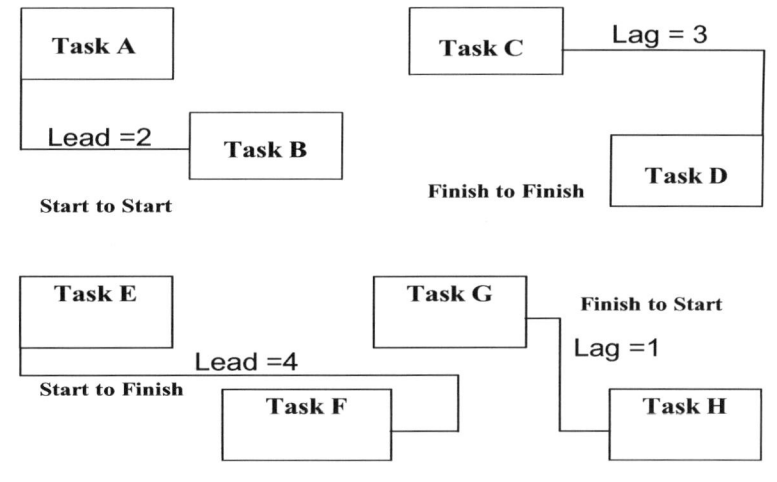

Figure 6.1 Precedence Relationships

6.1.2 Critical Path Analysis (CPA)

Critical path analysis comprises 3 steps.

1) The Forward Pass – from left to right

This pass calculates the earliest possible start and finish times for each task.

   Early Finish = Early Start + Duration

2) The Backward Pass – from right to left

This pass calculates the latest possible start and finish dates which will complete the schedule on time.

   Late Start = Late Finish - Duration.

3) Calculate Total Float

   Total Float = Late Finish – Early Finish or Late Start – Early Start

Total Float is defined as the amount of time an activity can be delayed or extended without affecting the total project duration (end date)

6.1.3 Node Convention

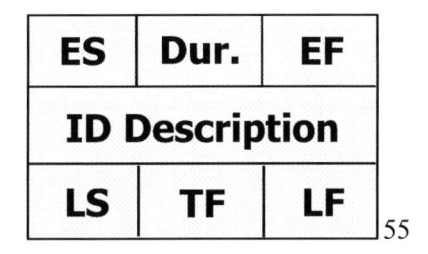

ES	Dur.	EF
ID Description		
LS	TF	LF

ES = Earliest Start Time
Dur = Activity Duration
EF = Earliest Finish Time
LS = Latest Start Time
TF = Total Float
LF = Latest Finish Time

6.1.4 Worked Example

Draw and completely analyse an activity-on-node network for the following project, assuming the project is to be completed in minimum time.

Activity	Duration	Dependency
A	10	NONE
B	15	A
C	5	A
D	8	A
E	2	D
F	10	B,C,E

Step 1- Construct the network and enter the durations

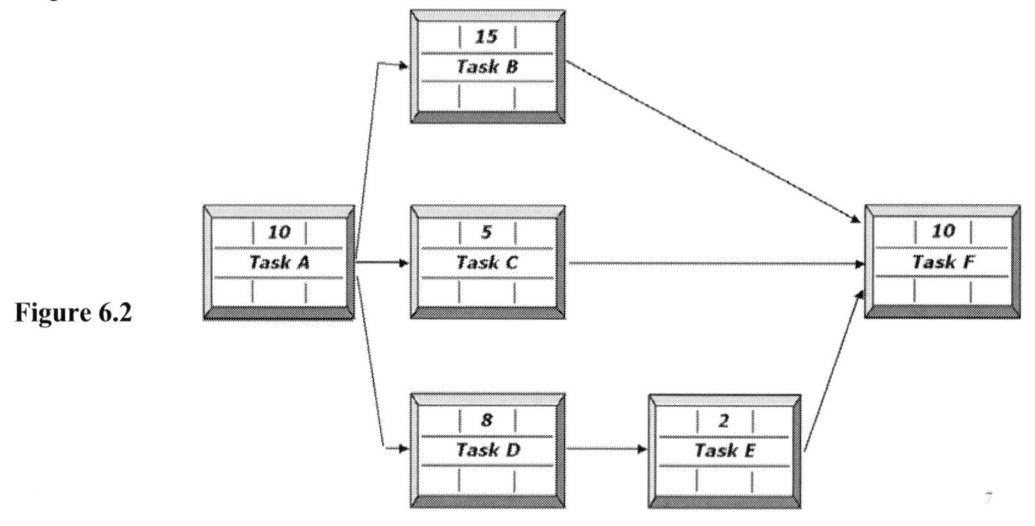

Figure 6.2

Step 2- Carry out the forward pass

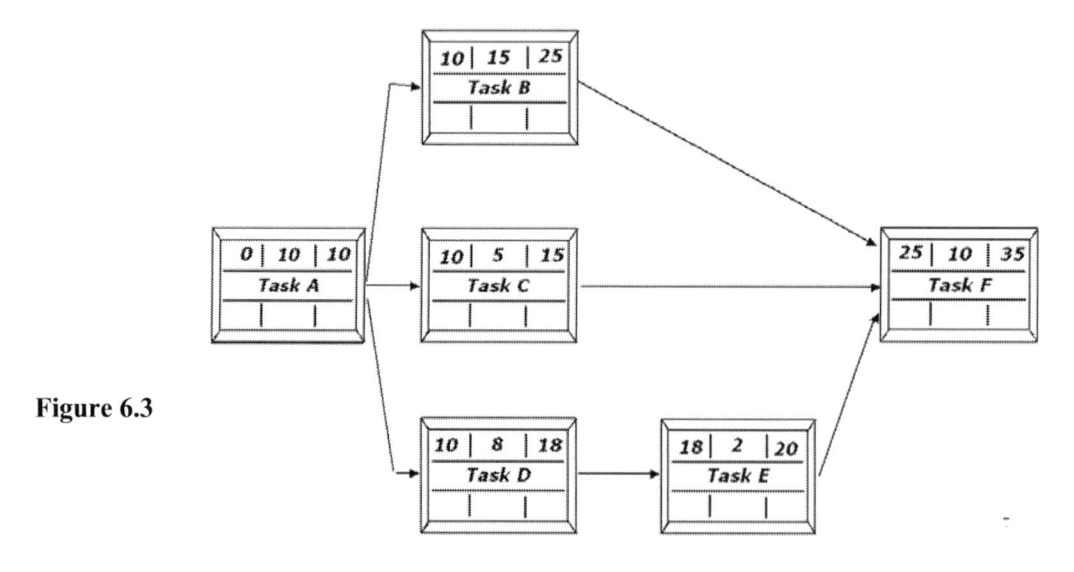

Figure 6.3

Thus for activity A, 0 + 10 = 10. This 10 is carried forward to all the successor activities and so on. Where there are multiple arrows we take the latest (the largest) as before. Thus for activity F we take the largest of 25 (from B), 15(from C) and 20(from E).

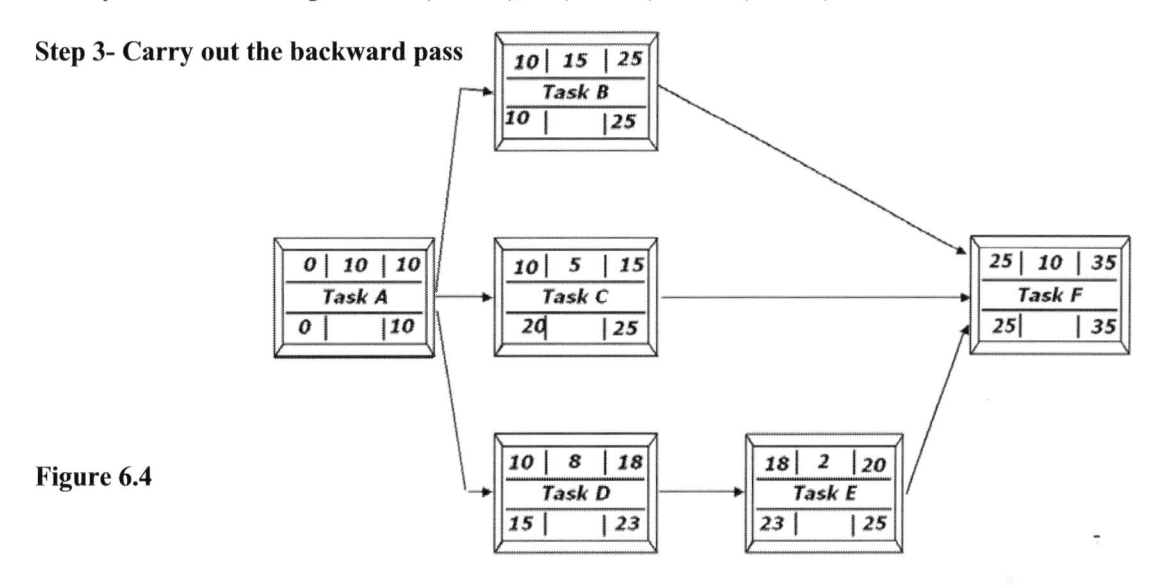

Step 3- Carry out the backward pass

```
          ┌─────────────┐
          │ 10 | 15 | 25│
          │   Task B    │
          │ 10 |    | 25│
          └─────────────┘
┌─────────────┐   ┌─────────────┐        ┌─────────────┐
│  0 | 10 | 10│   │ 10 |  5 | 15│        │ 25 | 10 | 35│
│   Task A    │──▶│   Task C    │───────▶│   Task F    │
│  0 |    | 10│   │ 20 |    | 25│        │ 25 |    | 35│
└─────────────┘   └─────────────┘        └─────────────┘
          ┌─────────────┐   ┌─────────────┐
          │ 10 |  8 | 18│   │ 18 |  2 | 20│
          │   Task D    │──▶│   Task E    │
          │ 15 |    | 23│   │ 23 |    | 25│
          └─────────────┘   └─────────────┘
```

Figure 6.4

Thus for activity F, 35(the finish time) – 10 (duration) = 25 (the start time)
This 25 becomes the latest finish date for B, C and E

Where there are multiple backward arrows e.g into activity A then we take the smallest which in this case is the 10 from B.

Step 4 Calculate Total Float by subtracting the early dates from the late dates.

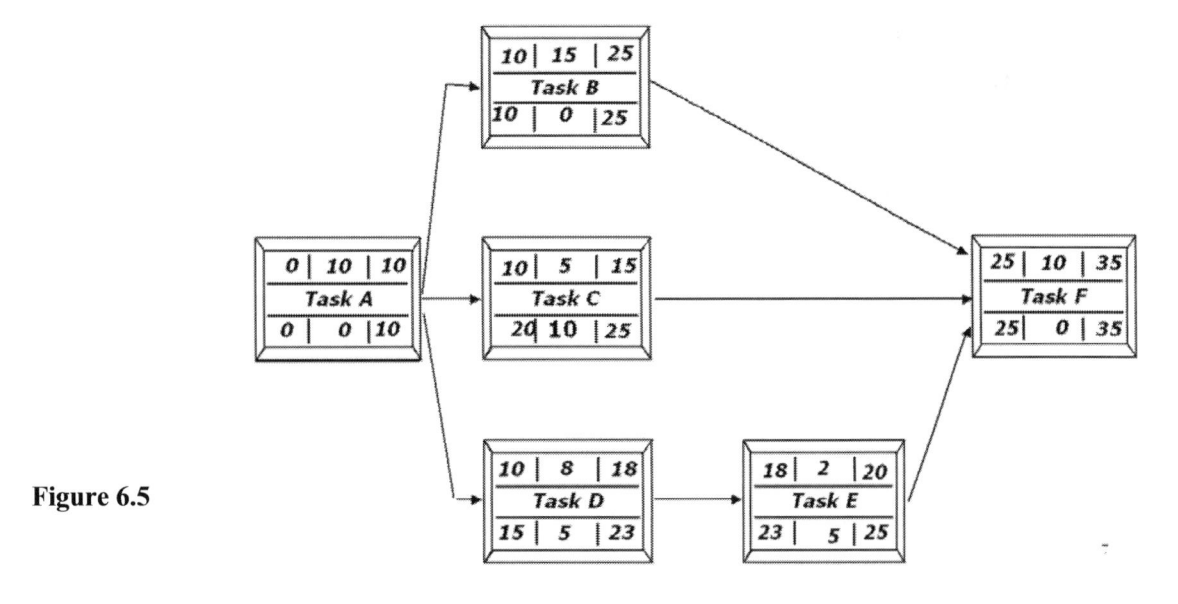

```
          ┌─────────────┐
          │ 10 | 15 | 25│
          │   Task B    │
          │ 10 | 0  | 25│
          └─────────────┘
┌─────────────┐   ┌─────────────┐        ┌─────────────┐
│  0 | 10 | 10│   │ 10 |  5 | 15│        │ 25 | 10 | 35│
│   Task A    │──▶│   Task C    │───────▶│   Task F    │
│  0 | 0 | 10 │   │ 20 | 10| 25 │        │ 25 | 0 | 35 │
└─────────────┘   └─────────────┘        └─────────────┘
          ┌─────────────┐   ┌─────────────┐
          │ 10 |  8 | 18│   │ 18 |  2 | 20│
          │   Task D    │──▶│   Task E    │
          │ 15 | 5 | 23 │   │ 23 | 5 | 25 │
          └─────────────┘   └─────────────┘
```

Figure 6.5

57

6.1.5 The Critical Path

The Critical path is the sequence of activities through a project network from start to finish, the sum of whose durations determines the overall project duration. On this path the late completion of activities will have an impact on the project end date.

The Critical Path is:-
- The longest path through the network
- The shortest possible planned project duration
- The path with least float

Thus in the above example the critical path is A>B>F

Knowledge of the Critical Path assists in the following areas:-

- To concentrate attention on activities which, if delayed, will affect project duration
- To identify non-critical activities which can be used to smooth forecast resource usage
- To identify 'near or sub critical' activities - those with very little float which require similar attention to critical activities
- To identify where resources can be switched between activities to maintain progress

6.1.6 Total Float and Free Float

Total Float is defined as the amount of time a task can be delayed without delaying the end date. **Free Float** is defined as the amount of time an activity can be delayed or extended without delaying the start of the next activity. The presence or absence of free float can be determined by inspection as the following example shows.

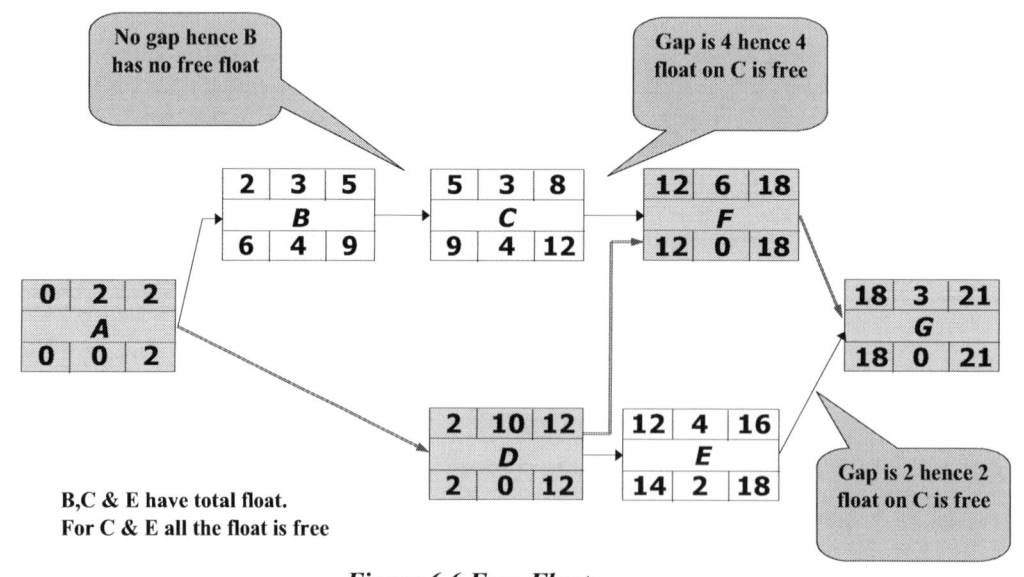

Figure 6.6 Free Float

The significance of Free Float is that the project manager knows that he can utilise free float to for instance ease temporary resource problems, knowing that there are no knock on effects. If there is total float but no free float then there will be knock on effects to consider. Also note that where a sequence of tasks in a line such as B,C above exhibit a value for total float then that float is effectively shared. If we utilise some or all of the total float in B then it will be removed from C. .

6.1.7 Gantt Charts

Strictly speaking a Gantt is just a series of bars, representing activities against a timeline which shows when activities take place. However the original concept has been extended to include logical connections which effectively means it is a network with the boxes drawn to a time scale. The figure below shows an example of a software generated Gantt chart.

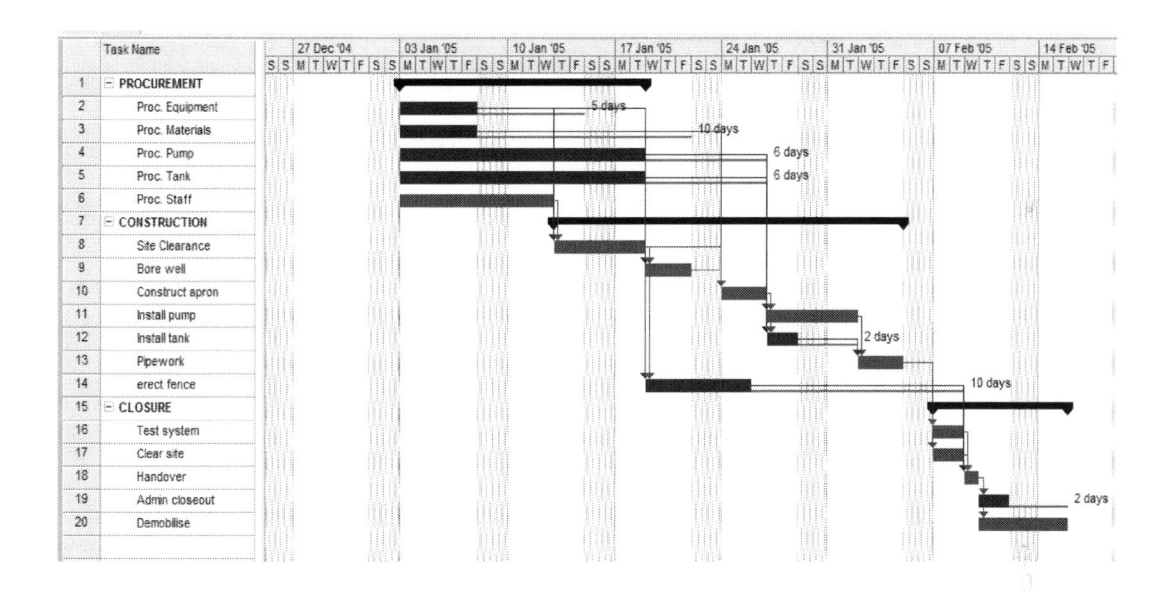

Figure 6.7 Software generated Gantt chart

6.1.8 Gantt Chart Features

Gantt charts are the most common way of representing a project schedule. They exhibit the following features

- A timeline shows the project calendar
- The length of a bar indicates duration
- Tasks are usually positioned at the earliest start date showing any float at the end
- Can be shown with or without logic connections (technically speaking a true Gantt chart does not show logical connections)
- Can also show comparison of current plan to original plan (baseline)

- Can be rolled up into summary tasks and can show milestones (key events, moments in time)
- Can be generated using software tools
- They are often simply referred to as Bar Charts

6.1.9 Gantt v Network

The following figure shows how a Gantt chart and a Precedence Network are effectively two ways of depicting the same situation

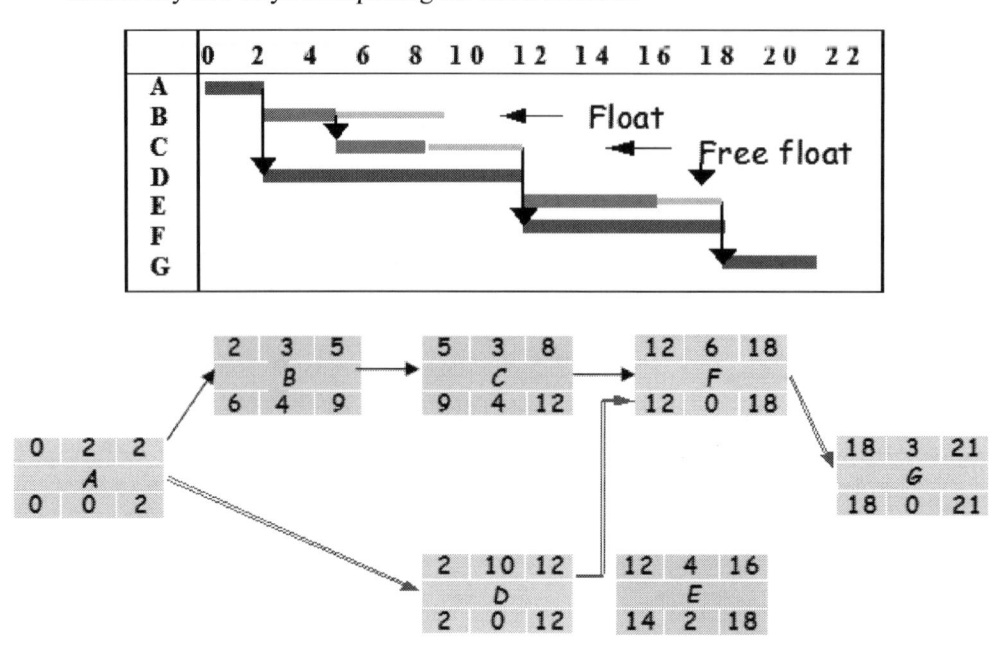

Figure 6.8 Comparison of Gantt and Network

6.1.10 Milestone Planning

Although it is usually necessary to plan in detail, in the early stages of a project such detail is not usually available and planning takes place at a less detailed level. We generally start by establishing the key milestones. Milestones are key occurrences in the project which mark the achievement of key objectives such as the completion of a phase. Milestones are used by management for project control. They are often not concerned with project detail but only in the progress against key milestones. Milestones are often linked to payment schedules. Completion of a milestone can trigger the issuing of an invoice.

6.1.11 Baselines

It is important that we are always able to compare actual achievement with the original plan. We must always retain a copy of the original plan. This is referred to as the baseline.

6.2 Resource Management

Resource Management is concerned mainly with people but also includes all project resources such as money and raw materials.

There are two principal classes of resources used on projects.

- **Consumable**s (Replenishable) - These can only be used once and must then be replenished. Examples include raw materials and money.
- **Re-usable** - Once no longer needed they are available for use elsewhere. Examples include machines, tools and of course people.

Resource Management is concerned with making resources available when required and avoiding waste. In the case of people it is better to have a smooth profile rather than continuous hire and fire. There are two methods for achieving this.

1. Time Limited Scheduling (Smoothing)
    This is usually the default option. Scheduling of resources will take place ignoring resource constraints. In other words infinite resource is assumed. This is usually the default option when doing the initial planning.

2. Resource Limited Scheduling (Levelling)
    No time limit is placed on the schedule. Tasks will take place at the earliest times resources become available.

6.3 Resource Smoothing

Resource smoothing attempts to resolve resource overloads by utilising Float. In this example utilising the float on activities C and E will not totally resolve the problem.

Consider the example here.

Figure 6.9

Resource Smoothing. Starting point

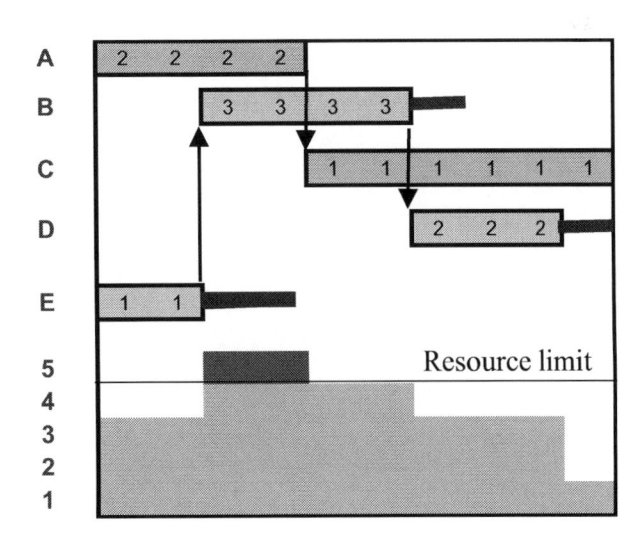

Applying **Resource Smoothing** and utilising the **float** on activity B and D we arrive at the position below. This is a **Time constrained schedule**. Here the network schedule is allowed to change but the end date is retained. *Resource Smoothing is time constrained.*

Time constrained schedule

In this case the network schedule is fixed and the program will allocate the required resource.

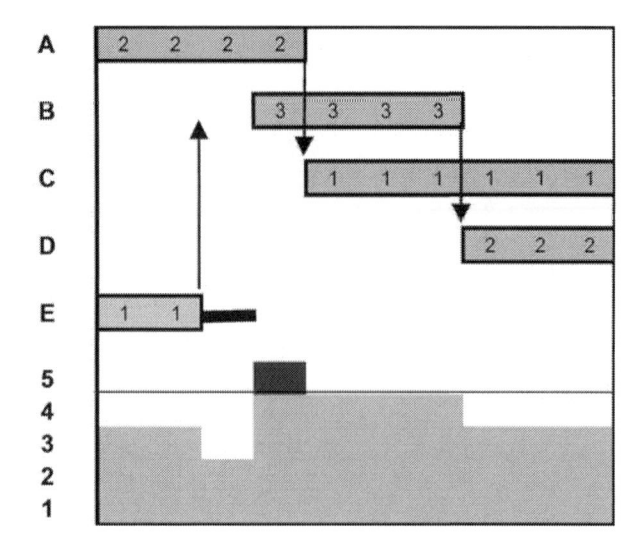

Figure 6.10   Resource Smoothing.-Finishing point

6.4   Resource Levelling

In order to fully address the resource overload, in this example we must delay B and hence D thus extending the project. This process of **Resource Levelling** is resource constrained and the outcome is shown below.

Resource Constrained Schedule

Levelling eliminates resource problems by ignoring time constraints.

It is **Resource** constrained

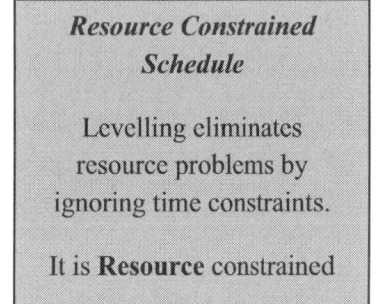

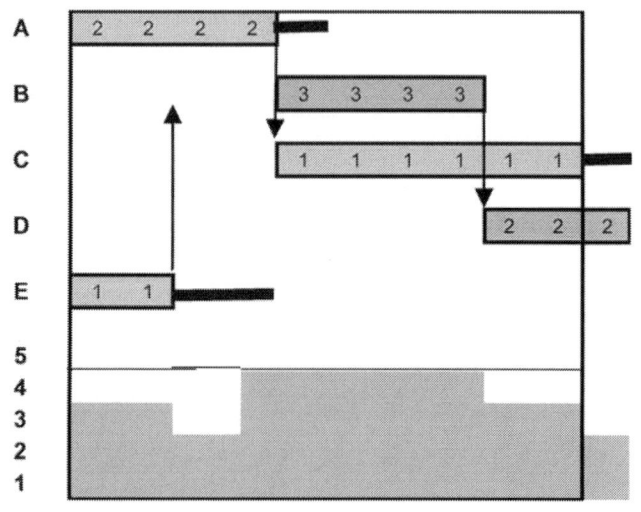

Figure 6.11 Resource Levelling

62

6.5 Procurement

6.5.1 Definitions

Procurement
The securing (or acquisition) of goods or services for use in your project.

Procurement (or Acquisition) Strategy
Determining the most appropriate means of procuring the component parts or services of a project

Contract
An agreement between two parties which is legally binding'

Contractor
A person, company or firm who holds a contract for carrying out the works and/or the supply of goods in connection with the Project

Supplier
Any organisation, including contractors and consultants, which supplies goods or services to customers.

6.5.2 The Procurement Process
The overall procurement process is illustrated in the flowchart below.

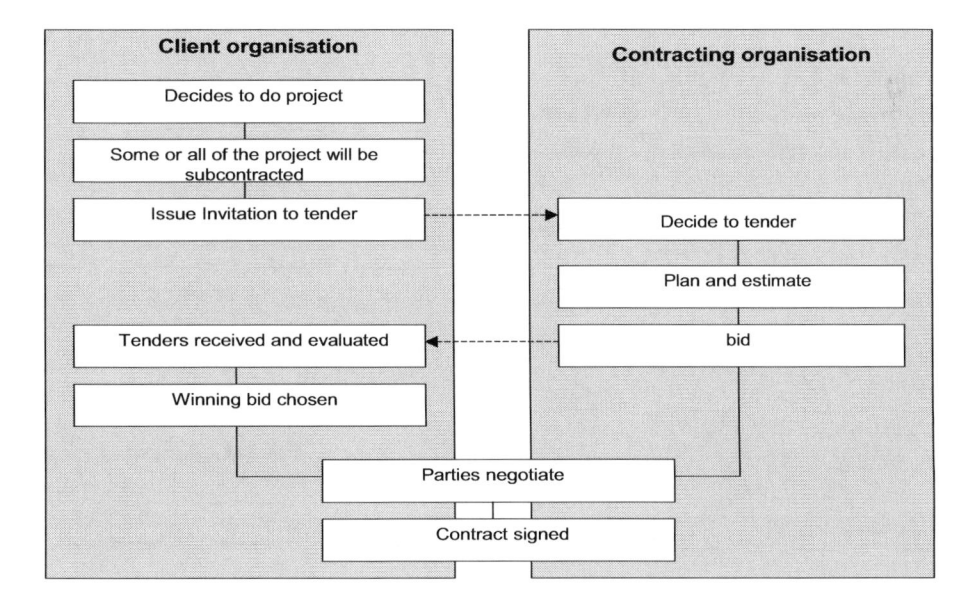

Figure 6.12 The Procurement Process

6.5.3 Procurement Strategy

Before an organisation issues an "Invitation to Tender" (ITT) it needs to consider a number of strategic issues that will affect the nature of the eventual contract. e.g.

- The initial make-or-buy decision based on a comparison of the actual costs and benefits of both options
- What form of contract will be used?
- How suppliers will be selected
- The kind of relationship required
- Whether to use a single supplier or multiple suppliers
- What will be the payment terms and pricing structure?

The answers to these questions will go a long way towards determining the most appropriate contract type.

6.5.4 Make or Buy

Many organisations have their own in-house capabilities so before procuring goods or services they must decide whether is is better to do it themselves. This is known as "Make or Buy Analysis". The analysis should include the following factors.

1. The direct costs of a prospective procurement.

2. The indirect costs – i.e. the cost of managing and monitoring the purchasing process

3. The overall effect of the decision on the organisation e.g. would a decision to **Make** have a knock on effect on other projects which may require the *same* resources. Would a decision to outsource put in-house facilities at risk?

7 Project Risk & Issue Management

Learning Objectives

- Understand the concept of risk as both a threat and an opportunity

- Describe the Risk Management process

- Explain the purpose and benefits of Risk Management

- Describe the use of a Risk Register

- Understand the difference between a Risk and an Issue

- Describe the use of an Issue Log

7.1 Definitions of Risk

APM definition:

"Combination of the probability or frequency of occurrence of a defined threat or opportunity and the magnitude of the consequence of the occurrence."

The above is more a statement of how risk is measured. A better definition is:-

A project risk is something that might occur, and if it does, will impact on the project's objectives of time, cost and performance/quality. Risk is uncertainty in an outcome. Risks can be both threats (downside) and opportunities (upside).

7.2 The Risk Management Plan

By their nature all projects are inherently risky; therefore the management of risk should an integral part of the project and carried out over the entire life cycle. Traditionally risks have been thought of solely as negative events but current thinking treats risk as uncertainty which can have positive or negative effects. The term "risk event" covers both threats and opportunities and both can be managed through a single process.

The way in which risk is to be managed in a project is detailed in the "**Risk Management Plan.**" The Risk Management Plan defines how all the risk processes will be carried out. It does not consider individual risks.

Risk management plan content

- The methodology and data sources
- Roles & responsibilities
- Budgeting for risk management
- Timing, i.e. when risk assessment will be carried out
- Qualitative and quantitative scoring methods
- Risk thresholds
- Reporting format
- How risks will be tracked

7.3 Risk Management Process

The purpose of risk management is to identify all significant risks to the project and manage those risks so as to eliminate or minimise threats, and maximise opportunities. The process is outlined in the diagram following (Fig 3.1).

Figure 3.1

The Risk Management Process

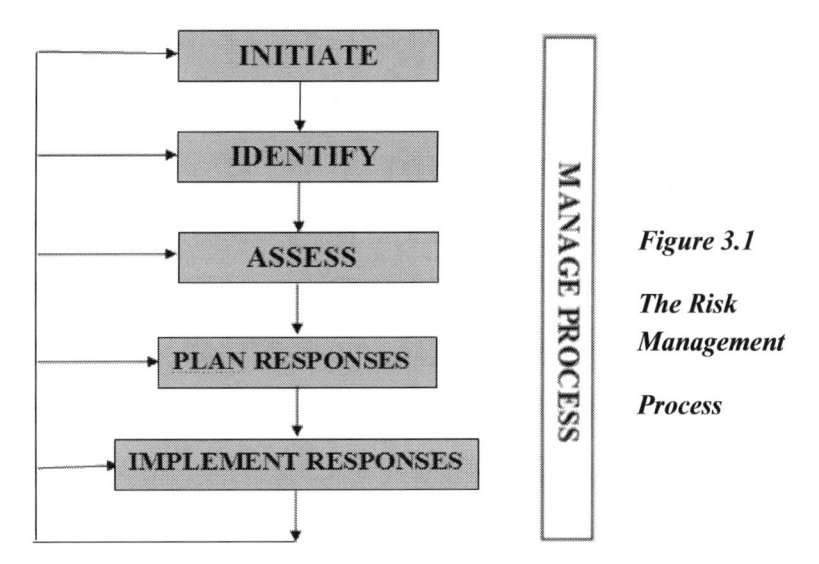

7.3.1 Initiation

This is the activity of setting up the process, making decisions on such things as risk categories and tools and techniques to be used. Basically it is about organising the team to carry out risk management.

7.3.2 Risk Identification

There are a variety of techniques for identification of risks events. e.g.

- **Brainstorming**
    - Using the project team and appropriate stakeholders
- **SWOT Analysis**
    - Strengths and Opportunities generate upside risks
    - Weaknesses and Threats identify downside risks
- **Assumptions Analysis**
    - Looking at the assumptions made in the planning to see if any of them constitute a risk
- **Constraints analysis**
    - Similarly for project constraints
- **Using the WBS**
    - Identifying risks to individual work packets
- **Interviews**
    - Interviewing people with knowledge or insight

There may also be sources of information external to the project that can help the identification process e.g.

- **Prompt/Check Lists**
    - Using existing prompt sheets and check lists
- **Post Project Reviews (Lessons learned)**
    - From previous projects with some commonality
- **Risk Registers of other projects**
    - Again, using projects with some commonality

7.3.3 Risk Assessment

The purpose of Risk Assessment is to prioritise the identified risks. In particular it needs to establish the key risks that require management focus.

Assessment is based on determining Probability and Impact and this is most conveniently carried out with the aid of a Probability and Impact Grid.

7.3.3.1 Probability and Impact Grid

The Probability and Impact Grid is a simple but effective tool that is used to prioritise identified risks. An example is illustrated below. In this instance we are using a scale that involves using judgement to place probability and impact from very low to very high.

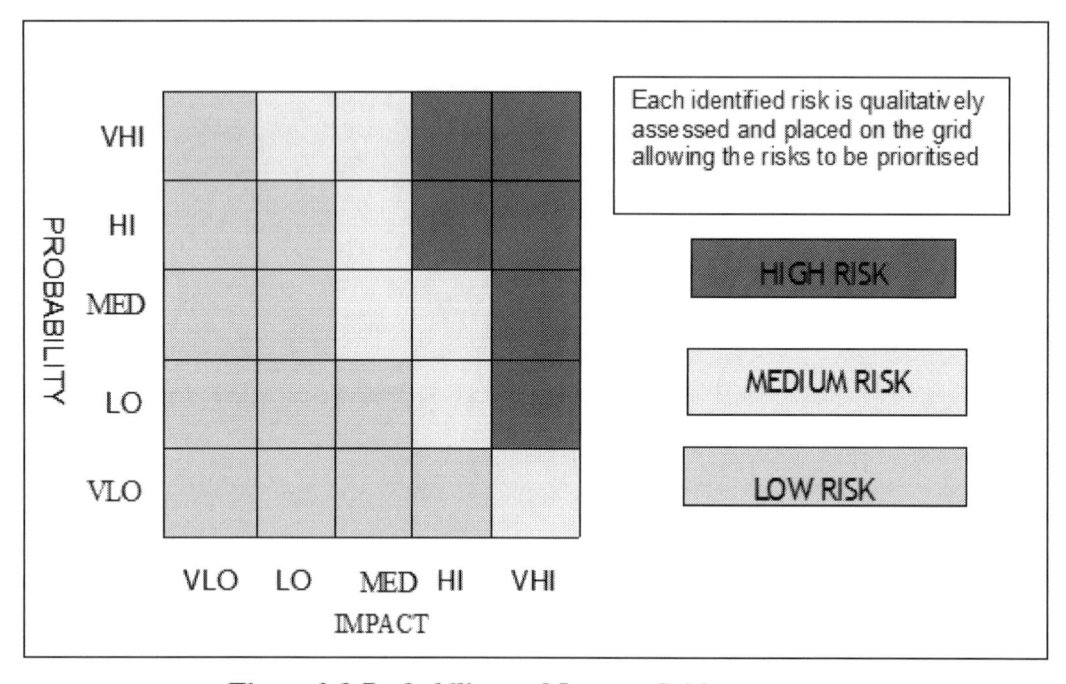

Figure 3.2 Probability and Impact Grid

7.3.3.2 Qualitative and Quantitative Analysis

The above assessment method is purely **Qualitative** in the sense that the scales are subjective assessments of the probability and impact. This is sufficient to prioritise the risks but for a full and proper assessment the analysis should be **Quantitative.** The probability grid can be converted to a quantitative method by stating probability and impact in numeric terms. There are also other quantitative techniques such as Monte Carlo methods and Decision Tree analysis but these are beyond the scope of this course.

A pseudo quantitative method often used is to simply apply a scale of 1 to 5 to the impact and probability. Multiplying these scales gives the ***Exposure*** for each square that can be used to prioritise the risks.

Exposure = Probability x Impact

A drawback of this method is that it gives the same weight to both probability and impact whereas in reality high impact is more serious than high probability. High impact items must be addressed even if they have low probability. The shading in the grid is a better representation of the relative importance.

	1	2	3	4	5
5	5	10	15	20	25
4	4	8	12	16	20
3	3	6	9	12	15
2	2	4	6	8	10
1	1	2	3	4	5

Figure 3.3

7.3.4 Risk Response Planning

Threats

There are 5 common strategies for addressing downside risks or threats. These are applied either individually or in combination.

1. **Avoid**
   Avoid the risk and eliminate uncertainty by not doing something or doing it in a different way
2. **Transfer**
   Transfer liability or ownership of a risk to someone else such as the client or sub-contractor or 3rd party. e.g. insurance or back to back contracts
3. **Reduce/Mitigate**
   If the risk cannot be avoided and is too large to accept then we must take steps to reduce probability and/or impact
4. **Accept**
   Take it on board and accept the consequences. The severity/probability of the risk does not justify great effort in managing it.
5. **Contingency Plan**
   Have an alternative plan at hand to implement if the risk occurs

When the severity of a risk determines that it must be actively managed then the following process should be followed:-

1. Re-examine the risk to determine its current status and validate the previous evaluation
2. Demonstrate the viability of the mitigation plan by evaluating the cost of mitigation and comparing with the reduction in exposure.
3. Decide if the mitigation results in an acceptable level of risk.
4. If so decide on who will own and manage the risk and be empowered to do so.

For any risk the person who manages that risk should be the person best placed to do so.

Opportunities

Similarly there are strategies for developing opportunities.

1. **Exploit**
   Try and exploit the opportunity by eliminating the uncertainties surrounding the opportunity
2. **Share**
   If you do not have the resources to exploit the opportunity yourself then try to find a partner to share it.
3. **Enhance**
   Work to increase the probability and impact of the opportunity
4. **Accept**
   Wait and see what happens

7.3.5 Implement Responses

Each risk that has a planned response must be proactively managed by the person responsible. In addition the risk plan needs to be formally reviewed on a regular basis.

The situation is bound to change because:-

- Some risks mature into problems (issues)
- Some risks are resolved or do not arise
- Probability/impacts change; up or down
- New risks arise that were not identified initially
- Project scope changes give new risk opportunities

The primary tool for managing risk is the Risk Register an example of which is shown below.

Project _____			Prepared by: _____	Reference:_____	
Key: H - High, M - Medium, L - Low				Date:_____	
Risk ID	Description	Prob H M L	Impact Cost Time	Response Strategy	Effect	Risk Owner

Figure 3.4 Example Risk register

The Risk Register must be routinely reviewed on a regular basis and when risk events happen. The overall risk status of the project and the progress of "active" risks will be reported as part of the standard project reporting procedures as defined in the Risk Management Plan and the Communications Plan.

7.3.6 The Benefits of Managing Risk

On many projects risks are not actively managed for the reasons stated later on. However as well as being a requirement of good **Governance,** the proper management of risk confers significant benefits.

- Increased understanding by the project leads to more realistic plans and greater probability of delivering to them. Increased understanding of the risks, leads to their minimisation and allocation to the person best placed to manage them. The understanding of risk helps determine the most appropriate contract type. A team view of the risks can lead to more objective decision making

- Financially and/or technically unsound/risky projects will be discouraged There will be a better understanding of the project by Stakeholders leading to increased confidence in the Project Management. It focuses management attention on the most significant threats to the project

7.3.7 Drawbacks of Managing Risk

The Cost

Risk Management is an overhead requiring a significant input of effort and cost. Although this is no different from the input of effort and cost into all Planning processes, such as Scope Management and Change Control, there is one key difference - Risk Management is about things that may never happen and even if they might, "it won't happen to me".

Visibility

Once we have put lots of effort and money into Risk Management the likely result is that it tells us what we didn't want to know. We will either have to invest in reducing the risks or accept that the project might take a lot longer, or cost a lot more than we had hoped or even that we should not do the project at all.

Many people may have a vested interest in the project and do not wish to hear anything that might endanger it.

7.4 *Issue Management*

APM define an Issue as a problem that cannot be solved by the project manager. *APM acknowledge that this is not a generally held definition.* A more universal definition of an issue is "a problem that requires immediate attention". However it is important in the exam that you adhere to the APM definition.

Some issues arise out of risks events that had been previously identified. Others will come as a complete surprise.

Some Issues may necessitate formal changes that require the Change Control Process to be invoked. For example a Client suddenly announces a major budget cut which necessitates reduction to project scope.

Some Issues will not cause a formal change but must be managed. For example a key resource resigns from the project or a vital piece of equipment breaks down.

It is important to have a formal process to manage issues. If they are caught earlier they should be easier to resolve before causing damage. The process is similar to Risk management

- **Identification**
    - By their very nature Issues tend to identify themselves
- **Escalation**
    - At what level in the project/organisation must this issue be addressed for a solution? Who owns the issue?
- **Monitoring**
    - The Owner monitors the issue and reports on progress. An Issue log is maintained.
- **Resolution**
    - The issue is closed when fully resolved to the satisfaction of all parties.

7.4.1 Issue Log

Once an Issue has been formally escalated it is entered onto the Issue Log which is very similar to the Risk register. In fact Issues can be thought of as Risks that were not previously identified or were accepted but have turned out more severe than expected or had a very low probability of occurrence.

Many organisations group risks and issues together and maintain a single Risks & Issues Register

8 Project Quality Management

Learning Objectives

- Describe what is meant by quality and quality management

- Understand the processes of quality planning, quality control and quality assurance

- Understand the distinction between quality assurance and quality control

- Define continuous improvement

8.1 Definition of Quality

Quality can be defined as the totality of characteristics of an entity that bear on its ability to satisfy stated or implied needs. A quality product must conform to the defined requirements/specifications but most importantly must be "fit for purpose".

Customer requirements are the basis for managing Quality. A "Quality" product is one that meets the specification and satisfies the customer.

"Over delivering" often called "Gold Plating" can be regarded as poor quality.

8.1.1 Quality V Grade

Quality must not be confused with Grade. Grade is to do with relative functionality and features. A high grade product may be rich in functionality and possibly luxury fittings but if it does not conform to requirements and meet customer expectations it is not a quality product. Conversely a product with basic, minimal functionality and lack of "frills" can be a quality product.

8.1.2 Elements of Quality Management

Quality Management is a management discipline concerned with making sure that activities happen according to a prescribed plan. It is all about preventing problems. Quality management involves carrying out a project through all its phases with zero deviations from the project specifications and adhering to defined processes.

The elements of Project Quality Management are:-

- **Quality Planning**
- **Quality Assurance**
- **Quality Control**

8.1.3 Quality Planning

Quality planning is defined as "identifying which quality standards are relevant to the project and determining how to apply and satisfy them". In other words, setting standards and how to achieve them. The primary output of the quality planning process is the Project Quality Management Plan. It describes how the project team intends to implement its Quality Policy. This reinforces the basis of modern thinking about project quality management; that is quality is a planned activity and not something that is applied afterwards by inspection and correction. Inspection still has a part to play in quality management; however increased inspection is not generally considered the best path to improved quality.

8.1.4 Quality Assurance

Quality Assurance is defined as the process of evaluating overall project performance on a regular basis to provide confidence that the quality system is being followed and project will satisfy the relevant quality standards.

The following items are part of quality assurance:

Formal Audits

- Project Audit
- Quality Audit - ISO 9000
- Financial Audit
- Technical Audit

Audits examine if processes, policies and procedures are being adhered to. Audits can be internal to the project, within the organisation but outside the projects or from external bodies. e.g checking for ISO 9000 compliance.

Reviews

Reviews can be more informal than audits. Thy concentrate more on what the project is producing and the project status and environment rather than the processes. Reviews should be constructive not destructive or people will be reluctant to participate.

8.1.5 Quality Control

Quality Control involves measuring project products to test if they conform to the relevant standards and also identifying ways to correct unsatisfactory performance and deviation from specification.

8.1.6 Quality Control v Quality Assurance

The basic difference between the two processes is that Quality Control is about doing the physical things to ensure quality in your product whilst Quality Assurance is concerned with checking that all the processes and procedures specified in the Quality Plan have been properly carried out. Quality Assurance is fundamentally an audit process. Whilst Quality Control is a project team activity Quality Assurance is carried out by external auditors as well as self auditing within the project team

8.1.7 Continuous Improvement

The Japanese word for continuous improvement is Kaizen. The philosophy espoused by kaizen is that quality comes from continuous minor improvements. It is the responsibility of both workers and management to always be on the lookout for ways to improve the quality of the finished product and the processes that produce it. This also can involve "Lean Thinking" which is concerned with continuously striving to reduce resources without adversely affecting quality and thus increasing productivity and profitability.

8.1.8 Project Management Responsibilities

Finally it must be stressed that the Project Manager carries overall responsibility for the quality of the project and the project deliverables.

The Project Manager should:

- Make sure that all project personnel are aware of the need for quality and the required quality standards and that they have received the necessary training and are capable of carrying out the work to the appropriate standard

- Make sure that there is an approved quality plan detailing all the required quality assurance and control procedures and standards and that all the project team and relevant stakeholders are familiar with the requirements of the plan.

- Make sure everyone is aware, by means of appropriate training and communication, of their roles & responsibilities for carrying out quality management actions. If necessary appoint a Quality Manager.

- Carry out monitoring and controlling actions to make sure that the product quality is being adhered to as per the quality plan, and that the outcomes of quality audits are noted and acted upon.

- Ensure there is an effective change control process in place and communicate regularly throughout the project with client and stakeholders to ensure that the project deliverables continue to be aligned with client requirements.

Remember that the modern attitude to quality is that it is built into the product and the people and processes that build it. Quality is not something that is achieved by inspection and correction. Quality is planned in. The motto is "Get it right 1st time"

9 Communication

Learning Objectives

- Understand the importance of effective project communications

- Outline the different media through which we can communicate

- Be aware of potential barriers to communication

- Define the content and benefits of the Communications Management Plan

9.1 Communications Management

Communications Management is concerned all the ways in which information is exchanged and interpreted. This is achieved in 3 main ways, written, verbal and by body language.

Written

Written communication is permanent. It is memory independent but can still be ambiguous and open to interpretation

E-mail, although written, has some of the elements of speech because it is immediate and it is easy to send something you may have cause to regret. However unlike speech or ordinary written communications it can literally be published to the world in minutes

Verbal

The majority of our communication is done this way. The advantage is that it is fast, easy and natural. However spoken words are transient and are easily misunderstood and may be recalled in different ways

Body Language

Body language can give away our feelings even when they contradict our words and can convey a message without using words.

9.2 Channels of Communication

Most of what a project manager does involves communication and there are innumerable channels of communication available, many of which make increasing use of technology.

Examples

- Meetings
- Presentations
- Telephone
- One to one
- Video Conferencing
- Text messaging
- Newsletters
- Contracts
- Websites

- Blogs
- e-mails
- Progress Reports
- Fax
- Letters
- Drawings
- Specifications
- Internet
- Publications

9.3 Barriers to Communication

There are many things that can get in the way of the transmission and reception of a message. The following are examples of these barriers to communication.

9.3.1 Environmental Barriers
These are barriers that arise from the environment in which the communication is taking place. e.g

- Noise distractions
- Too high or low temperature
- Poor air quality
- Visual distractions
- The medium
- Information overload

9.3.2 Background
We filter the words of others based upon our technical, social and educational background e.g.

- Jargon
- Culture
- Language
- Social class
- Financial status

9.3.3 Personal
This involves things personal to ourselves. e.g.

- Tiredness
- Hunger
- Thirst
- Personal prejudice
- Preconceptions
- Stereotyping
- Culture

9.3.4 Organisational
This is to do with factors within your organisation .e.g

- Relative seniority
- Security
- Company culture

9.4 Effective Communications

The ability to communicate is probably the most important skill a project manager possesses. The following factors will greatly enhance the effectiveness of communications.

- Always use the most appropriate means to communicate
- Ask for and give feedback
- Be aware of blockers and barriers
- Do not be a communications bottleneck
- Use standard reporting formats
- Use exception reporting
- Keep all stakeholders aware of important events/changes
- Restrict meetings to appropriate personnel
- Have a Communications Management Plan
- Hold effective meetings

9.5 Importance of effective communications planning

- Project staff must know what their tasks are and how to accomplish them otherwise no progress will be made

- Team leader and the PM must know what the project staff are doing otherwise they cannot monitor project progress.

- You must keep your client/sponsor aware of project status and manage their expectation otherwise you may not be doing what they want you to do

- You must maintain channels of communication with project staff and stakeholders so that everyone knows what is going on and the work of the project can carry on in a fully integrated and co-ordinated manner

- An effective plan will ensure that everyone will receive the same, accurate, timely information. This will help avoid mistakes and delays

- If good communication are not in place then people will make incorrect assumptions

9.6 The Communications Management Plan

On any project informal communication will arise naturally. However much of the required communication is formal and should be properly planned and documented in a Communications Management Plan. This plan should do the following:-

- Detail and describe all the project information requirements
- Detail means of acquiring information

- Describe the methods by which information will be stored
- Describe how information will be secured and access to it controlled
- Describe a distribution system that details to whom information will flow including format, content and level of detail
- Establish the project reporting structure
- Provide schedules showing when each type of communication will be produced and to whom it is sent (see example of Communications Matrix below)
- Describe methods for updating information

Key
W - Weekly
M - Monthly
Q - Quarterly
A - As required

	Sponsor/ Board	Client Manager	Programme Manager	Project Manager	Functional Managers	Project Office	Manager	User Representative	Team Leaders	Project Team
Project Plan										
Change Log										
Risk register										
Project Status										
Project Schedule										
Milestone report										
Etc etc										

Figure 9.1 Communications Matrix

10 Teamwork and Leadership

Learning Objectives

- Define what is meant by Leadership

- Define what is meant by the term project team

- Describe how a leader can influence team performance

- Understand the advantages and disadvantages of using team models

10.1 The Project Manager as Leader

Project managers are expected to plan, manage and organise but the most important skill is Leadership. Leadership is mainly based on example and good communication skills

10.1.1 Attributes of Good Leaders

- Lead by example-are Role Models
- Are good communicators, especially listening
- Are seen to be fair and even handed
- Are good at the other aspects of project management
- Command respect
- Care about people
- Will take risks for, and stand up for their people
- Will always be there for the team
- Know what is going on

Good leaders lead by example. Team members are greatly influenced by the behaviour of the leader. They will take their lead from the project manager and will tend to pick up both good and bad behaviour.

10.1.2 Leadership Activities

Give Feedback

Even though team members may only work for you on a temporary basis and have their own line manager the PM must still provide constructive feedback to enable people to develop their skills and improve on their weak areas

Recognise Achievement

People expect hard work and achievement to be recognised. They also require a record of that recognition so do it in writing.

Reward Success

Recognition is essential but people also expect to be rewarded. Public recognition is a form of reward but eventually rewards must be tangible.

Encourage, Support and Motivate

A good leader will spend time coaching and encouraging people to become more effective and will always support his team members.

Set Realistic Goals & Objectives

The setting of individual and team goals is a key activity. Goals must be challenging but not so difficult as to become de-motivating. Individual goals must be compatible and aligned with the needs of the project.

Be Available

Finally a good leader will make sure he is available to his team and maximises face to face contact. This can be difficult to achieve on geographically dispersed projects.

10.1.3   Leadership Styles (Hersey & Blanchard)

Hersey and Blanchard developed what they called a *Situational Leadership Model*.
In simple terms, a situational leader is one who can adopt different leadership styles depending on the situation.

They defined 4 basic leadership styles for getting tasks done:-

1. Directing
2. Coaching
3. Supporting
4. Delegating

These four styles can be expressed in terms of *Supporting Behaviour* (concern for the person) and *Directive Behaviour* (concern for the task).

This is illustrated following:-

	Supporting	**Coaching**
High	Leader facilitates and takes part in decisions, but day to day control is with the follower.	Leader defines roles and tasks of the follower and supervises closely. Communication is largely one way.
Supporting Behaviour (Concern for the Person)	**Delegating**	**Directing**
	Leader sets direction then stands back. The follower decides when and how the leader will be involved	Leaders define roles and tasks of the 'follower', and supervise them closely. Decisions are made by the leader. Communication is largely one-way.
	Low — Directive Behaviour (Concern for the Task) — High	

10.2 The Project Team

10.2.1   A Team Definition

> *".. two or more people who interact, dynamically, interdependently, and adaptively toward a common and valued goal/objective/ mission, who have each been assigned specific roles or functions to perform"*
> Salas, Dickenson, Converse and Tannenbaum

Project teams are normally transient and will be disbanded upon completion of the project.

10.2.2   Characteristics of Effective Teams

- They have a good leader
- There is a good blend of skills and personalities
- Team morale and motivation is high
- The team works together and everyone participates actively and positively in meetings and activities
- Everyone knows their own role in the team
- Team goals are given realistic time frames.
- Everyone is focused on the ultimate goal of the project
- Team goals are understood by everyone.
- Everyone is supportive of the project and of others
- There is trust between team members

10.3 Team models

Behavioural scientists have developed models of team dynamics to try and understand how people of different aptitudes and attitudes work together in teams. The two best known are Belbin and Margerison & McCann. The two are very similar in concept so only Belbin will be described in detail here. .

10.3.1   Belbin Roles

Dr. Raymond Meredith Belbin carried out research in the sixties on how people work within teams. He concluded that there were eight role types within a team and that team work better if all of those roles are represented in the team. This does not mean that a team must have 8 people because most people can adopt more than one role even though one role is often strongest.

Certain roles work well together and others not so well. There is a simple written test which purports to tell which roles a person is best suited for. This is useful information for a project manager. However with experience and knowledge of the role types it is possible to accurately determine role types without the test.

Belbin later added a ninth role, that of specialist brought in purely for their expert knowledge in a particular area.

The roles are illustrated below.

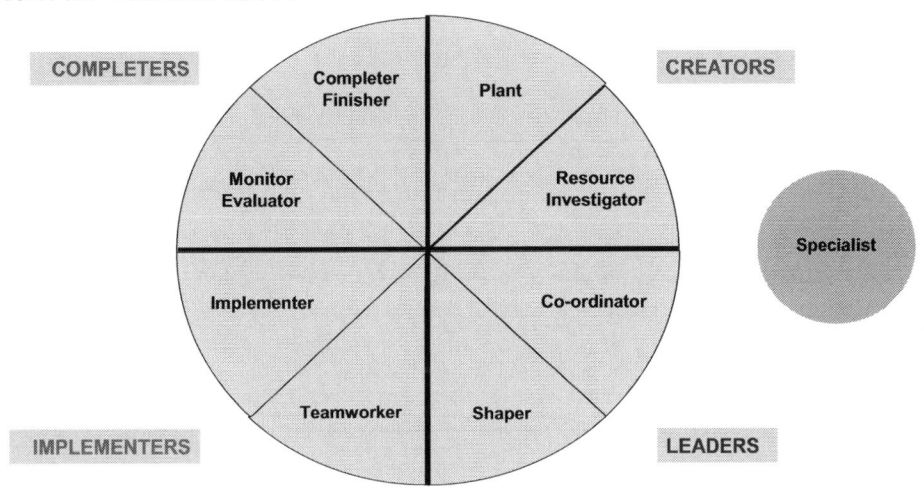

Figure 10.1 Belbin Roles

The roles are briefly described in the table following along with their weaknesses

Team Role	Description	Allowable Weaknesses	Not Allowable
Coordinator	Mature, confident, clarifies goals	Manipulative, lazy (own work)	Take credit for teams work
Shaper	Challenging, full of drive dynamic	Provokes others, hurts feelings	No apologies, no humour
Monitor Evaluator	Sober, strategic, sees options	Lacks drive, overly critical	Cynicism without logic
Team worker	Cooperative, mild, diplomatic	Indecisive, easily influenced	Avoiding pressure situations
Plant	Creative, unorthodox	Ignores details, preoccupied	Ownership vs. cooperation
Implementer	Disciplined, reliable, practical	Inflexible, slow to respond	Obstructing change
Completer / finisher	Painstaking, conscientious	Inclined to worry, nit-picker	Obsessive behaviour
Resource investigator	Develop contacts, enthusiastic	Overoptimistic, loses interest	Letting clients down
Specialist	Single minded, rare knowledge	Overlooks big picture	Ignoring important info.

10.3.2 Advantages & disadvantages

In the examination you will not be expected to have memorised the different roles. It concentrate on general principles and the advantages and disadvantages of using such models as Belbin and Margerison/McCann.

Both models work by testing people to find out which team roles they are best suited to. This enables people to be placed in roles they are most likely to enjoy. When people are matched to a role suitable for them they are likely to be happier in their job and perform better. It avoids the square peg in a round hole syndrome. So the principal advantage of using such models is having a motivated, happier and higher performing team. People forced into unsuitable roles will exhibit stress and performance and team morale will suffer.

The downside is that the process can be expensive and time consuming. It is also subject to manipulation if people being tested are aware of the method.

10.4 Team Building

When teams work together, and support each other, the team is much more than the sum of its parts. The team consists of a diverse collection of individuals with widely differing backgrounds, abilities, needs, and interests. Team members are initially unfamiliar with project goals and individuals' capabilities are unknown to the project manager. In addition matrix management mode makes it hard to obtain real commitments from team members who may work on the project part-time and/or temporary. Team building should be very high on a project manager's priority list and be a continuous activity. It is very easy to spot a poor performing team. It will exhibit some or all of the following symptoms.

- Frustration
- Unhealthy conflict
- Unproductive meetings
- Lack of trust in the PM

The results of good team building are also very apparent.

- Members are ready to work to a common goal
- There is team loyalty and identification
- Members are willing to work hard for the good of the team
- They are willing to sacrifice personal interests for the team good
- Team morale is high

10.5 Stages in Team Development

The most widely used model of team development is the "Forming, Storming, Norming, Performing model". This model is illustrated below.

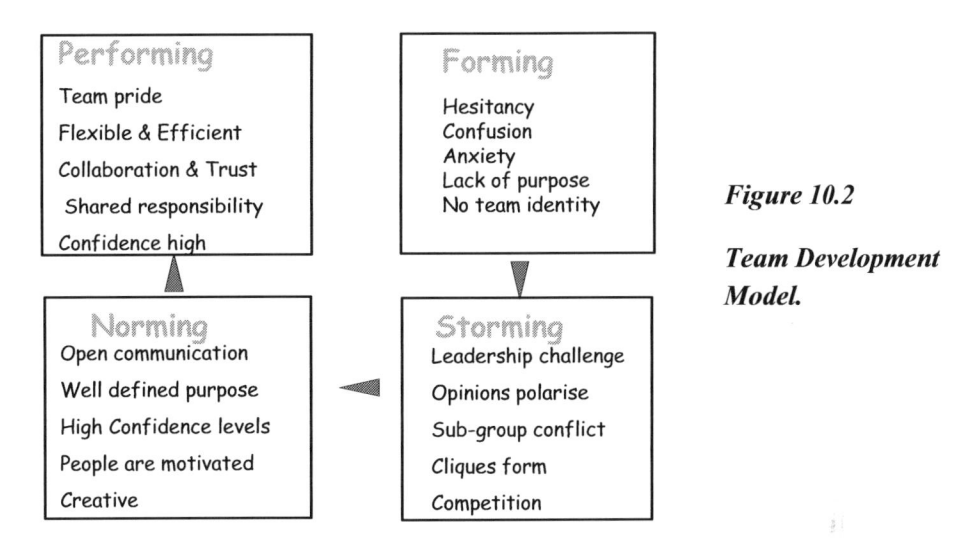

Performing
- Team pride
- Flexible & Efficient
- Collaboration & Trust
- Shared responsibility
- Confidence high

Forming
- Hesitancy
- Confusion
- Anxiety
- Lack of purpose
- No team identity

Norming
- Open communication
- Well defined purpose
- High Confidence levels
- People are motivated
- Creative

Storming
- Leadership challenge
- Opinions polarise
- Sub-group conflict
- Cliques form
- Competition

Figure 10.2

Team Development Model.

This is a well-recognised process that all teams go through. The job of the PM is to get the team performing and keep them there. The PM must also realise that going through the stages from Norming to Performing is natural and must be expected, Events such as team changes, change in objectives, uncontrolled changes or setbacks can cause a team to stop performing and revert to storming.

The way in which the model relates to project activities and what must take place to progress from one stage to the next is illustrated below.

Forming → Storming
Occurs during Concept/Initiation.
Business Plan-Milestone-Org. Structure

Storming → Norming
Associated with detailed Planning stage.
WBS-Schedule-RASCI chart-Risk Plan

Norming → Performing
Associated with Execution & Control
EV Management-Risk Management
Change Control etc

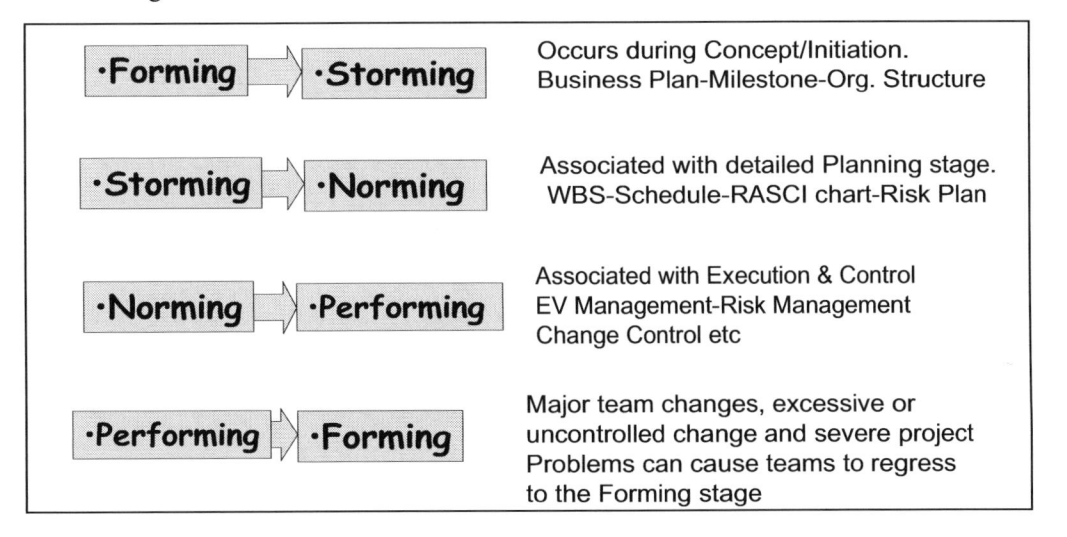

Performing → Forming
Major team changes, excessive or uncontrolled change and severe project Problems can cause teams to regress to the Forming stage

Figure 10.3 Stage Progression

10.6 Effective Team Building

Team building must be planned by the PM and become an integral part of the process of project management.

- Hold a kick off meeting at the start of the project
- Make sure everyone contributes to and "buys in" to the project plan
- Make sure everyone knows exactly what is expected of them.
- Understand, support and coach each individual
- Hold regular team building events.
- Praise in public, reprimand in private
- Provide motivation, reward and recognition
- Provide for skills development
- Shield your team from outside interference
- Celebrate successes and commiserate setbacks...as a team

11 Practice Questions

1. Which of the following statements is the most important responsibility of the project sponsor?

A. Monitoring daily progress of the project
B. Monitoring the project team's productivity
C. Ensuring the benefits of the project are realised.
D. Leading project evaluation reviews for lessons learned.

2. Which of the following best defines a portfolio?

A. All the Programmes carried out by an Organisation
B. All the Programmes and Projects carried out by an Organisation
C. All the Products and Services offered by an Organisation
D. All the Projects, Programmes and Operational activities carried out by an Organisation

3. Which of the following statements about a project life cycle is not true?

A. It consists of a number of distinct phases.
B. The number of phases can vary.
C. It has phases which should be roughly the same size.
D. Phasing facilitates the use of gateways.

4. Resource smoothing should:

A. Work within pre-determined resource levels.
B. Resolve resource overloads by utilising Float
C. Extend the activity duration.
D. Utilise overtime where necessary.

5. Which of the following would you not expect to find in a business case.

A. Project success criteria
B. Outline schedule
C. Stakeholder analysis
D. Detailed cash flow statement

6. Good leadership is all about:

A. Motivating people to be more effective.
B. Looking for opportunities rather than threats.
C. Getting people to understand what is best for them.
D. Letting people learn from their own mistakes.

7. Which of the following best describes a project's business case?

A. A list of the project deliverables and their costs.
B. The reason why the project should proceed.
C. A statement of all the estimated project costs and benefits.
D. A statement of all the project costs and benefits with detailed budgets and schedules.

8. Key Performance Indicators are used to monitor which of the following?

A. Success Criteria
B. Individual team member performance
C. Success Factors
D. Project progress

9. Which of the following is the best definition of a programme?

A. A group of projects which contribute to a strategic business objective.
B. A group of projects that are managed by one project manager.
C. All the projects within an organisation.
D. All the projects within the total organisation's portfolio.

10. Which of the following is the best definition of the critical path?

A. The shortest path from start to finish.
B. The path with the zero float.
C. The path with the largest number of activities.
D. The longest path through the network.

11. Configuration management is primarily concerned with:

A. Ensuring that the final product meets the needs of the business.
B. Minimising the impact of changes on the scope of the project.
C. Making sure that all changes are beneficial.
D. Ensuring the traceability and integrity of the delivered product or products

12. The primary purpose of a gate review is to:

A. Check on project status.
B. Check on project team performance.
C. Decide whether to continue with the next phase of the project.
D. Approve the plan for the next phase.

13. Which of the following statements best describes procurement?

A. All the activities concerned with negotiating with potential suppliers of goods and services.
B. The placing of a contract with a supplier.
C. Arranging for the supply and delivery of purchased goods to a project site.
D. The securing (or acquisition) of goods or services.

14. Project context can be defined as:

A. The business environment in which it takes place.
B. The technical difficulties of the project being undertaken.
C. Its potential impact on the environment.
D. Factors within the business environment that could affect the project.

15. A principal purpose of a project handover is:

A. To complete the project audit trail.
B. To pass legal responsibility and ownership to the client.
C. To verify that the project deliverables are fit for purpose.
D. To establish operational runn9ing of the product or service.

16. Which of the following statements is false?

A. A project sponsor should "champion" the project.
B. A project sponsor is responsible for the production of the project plan.
C. A project sponsor should have influence across functional boundaries.
D. A project sponsor should have some knowledge of project management.

17. Using the Work Breakdown Structure (WBS) to assist estimating is known as:

A. Comparative estimating.
B. Bottom-up estimating.
C. Definitive estimating.
D. Parametric estimating.

18. People interested in or affected by a project are called:

A. Bystanders
B. Key players
C. Stakeholders
D. Supporters

19. Which of the following best defines team work?

A. A group of people communicating effectively with each other
B. A group of people working collaboratively towards a common goal.
C. A group of people sharing a common goal.
D. A group of people working under the same leader

20. Which of the following is not a component of quality management?

A. Quality planning
B. Quality control
C. Quality measurement
D. Quality assurance.

21. The document that represents the prime means of communicating the project manager's intentions to the stakeholders is the:

A. Monthly project report.
B. Stakeholder management plan
C. Status audit report.
D. Project management plan.

22. Which of the following would not be classified as a project risk?

A. This project is outside our normal area of expertise.
B. We might not have sufficient people with the right experience to undertake the project.
C. We always find that initial planning takes longer than we thought.
D. We have never worked in that country before.

23. The business case is owned by:

A. The project manager.
B. The programme manager
C. The project sponsor.
D. The project board.

24. According to APM which of the following best describes a project issue?

A. A future risk that could have a significant negative impact.
B. A previously unidentified risk.
C. A routine project problem
D. A problem which cannot be resolved by the project manager.

25. Portfolio management is particularly helpful in managing:

A. Multiple interconnecting projects.
B. Resource conflicts.
C. Projects requiring multiple skills.
D. Risks to ongoing operations.

26. Responsibility for producing the project management plan lies with:

A. The project sponsor assisted by the project manager
B. The project manager assisted by the project sponsor.
C. The project manager and appropriate project team members.
D. The project planner.

27. Which of the following is true with regard to project quality?

A. Having a quality system will ensure that all products are of the approved standard.
B. Project quality is primarily the responsibility of people actually doing the work.
C. Quality cannot be achieved just by quality control inspections.
D. Quality will follow if everyone follows the quality system.

28. Which process determines if the quality system is being adhered to?

A. Design reviews
B. Project reviews
C. Quality audits
D. Product testing

29. A common acronym for an analysis of project context is:

A. PETAL
B. PASTEL
C. PISTOL
D. PESTLE

30. Which of the following best defines a portfolio?

A. The totality of all the projects, programmes and associated operations within an organisation
B. All projects and programmes within an organisation
C. A set of independent projects under the control of one manager
D. A +C

12   Practice Questions Answers

1. Which of the following statements is the most important responsibility of the project sponsor?

A. Monitoring daily progress of the project
B. Monitoring the project team's productivity
C. Ensuring the benefits of the project are realised.
D. Leading project evaluation reviews for lessons learned.

```
See page 25 paragraph 3.4.1. "Make sure business benefits
are realised"
```

2. Which of the following best defines a portfolio?

A. All the Programmes carried out by an Organisation
B. All the Programmes and Projects carried out by an Organisation
C. All the Products and Services offered by an Organisation
D. All the Projects, Programmes and Operational activities carried out by an Organisation

```
See Page 11 paragraph 1.7 "In a total business context a
portfolio is defined as the totality of all an
organisation's programmes, projects and related
operational activities".
```

3. Which of the following statements about a project life cycle is not true?

A. It consists of a number of distinct phases.
B. The number of phases can vary.
C. It has phases which should be roughly the same size.
D. Phasing facilitates the use of gateways.

```
Phases can be of any size depending on the project.
```

4. Resource smoothing should:

A. Work within pre-determined resource levels.
B. Resolve resource overloads by utilising Float
C. Extend the activity duration.
D. Utilise overtime where necessary.

> See page 61 paragraph 6.3
> "Resource smoothing attempts to resolve resource overloads by utilising Float"

5. Which of the following would you not expect to find in a business case

A. Project success criteria
B. Outline schedule
C. Stakeholder analysis
D. Detailed cash flow statement

> See page 30 paragraph 4.1.2 Cash flow is not included because it is far too early to consider such detail.

6. Good leadership is all about:

A. Motivating people to be more effective.
B. Looking for opportunities rather than threats.
C. Getting people to understand what is best for them.
D. Letting people learn from their own mistakes.

> See page 84 paragraph 10.1.2. "A good leader will spend time coaching and encouraging people to become more effective."

7. Which of the following best describes a project's business case?

A. A list of the project deliverables and their costs.
B. The reason why the project should proceed.
C. A statement of all the estimated project costs and benefits.
D. A statement of all the project costs and benefits with detailed budgets and schedules.

> See page 30 paragraph 4.1.1. "It must show the expected costs and benefits of the project……."

8. Key Performance Indicators are used to monitor which of the following?

A. Success Criteria
B. Individual team member performance
C. Success Factors
D. Project progress

> See page 33 paragraph 4.2.3 "Key Performance Indicators are continuously measured over the life of the project. They directly measure the project performance against Project Success Criteria"

9. Which of the following is the best definition of a programme?

A. A group of projects which contribute to a strategic business objective.
B. A group of projects that are managed by one project manager.
C. All the projects within an organisation.
D. All the projects within the total organisation's portfolio.

> See page 10, paragraph 1.6 "A Programme is a group of projects that are inter-related and/or interdependent and contribute to a common strategic objective."

10. Which of the following is the best definition of the critical path?

A. The shortest path from start to finish.
B. The path with the zero float.
C. The path with the largest number of activities.
D. The longest path through the network.

> See page 58, paragraph 6.1.5. Note that the critical path is not defined by zero float, but by least float. It is possible for the whole project have float. In this case each critical path activity will have a positive value for total float.

11. Configuration management is primarily concerned with:

A. Ensuring that the final product meets the needs of the business.
B. Minimising the impact of changes on the scope of the project.
C. Making sure that all changes are beneficial.
D. Ensuring the traceability and integrity of the delivered product or products

> See page 51, paragraph 5.9 "Controlling the configuration during the project will ensure the traceability and integrity of the delivered product or products."

12. The primary purpose of a gate review is to:

A. Check on project status.
B. Check on project team performance.
C. Decide whether to continue with the next phase of the project.
D. Approve the plan for the next phase.

```
See page 19, paragraph 2.4.1 "At each gateway the project
manager must report back to the project board or sponsor
and ask for authority to "pass through the gate" i.e.
proceed to the next phase."
```

13. Which of the following statements best describes procurement?

A. All the activities concerned with negotiating with potential suppliers of goods and services.
B. The placing of a contract with a supplier.
C. Arranging for the supply and delivery of purchased goods to a project site.
D. The securing (or acquisition) of goods or services.

```
See page 63, paragraph 6.5.1 "Procurement-The securing (or
acquisition) of goods or services"
```

14. Project context can be defined as:

A. The business and technical environment in which it takes place.
B. The technical difficulties of the project being undertaken.
C. Its potential impact on the environment.
D. Anything that could affect the project.

```
See page 14, paragraph 1.9. "Each project takes place in
its own particular business and technical
environment................"
```

15. A principal purpose of a project handover is:

A. To complete the project audit trail.
B. To pass legal responsibility and ownership to the client.
C. To verify that the project deliverables are fit for purpose.
D. To establish operational running of the product or service.

> See page 21, paragraph 2.5. "Handover consists of all those activities involved with the formal transfer of ownership from the project team to the client/sponsor and end users."

16. Which of the following statements is false?

A. A project sponsor should "champion" the project.
B. A project sponsor is responsible for the production of the project plan.
C. A project sponsor should have influence across functional boundaries.
D. A project sponsor should have some knowledge of project management.

> See page 36, paragraph 4.4. "It (the Project Management Plan) is owned by the Project Manager and approved by the Sponsor. Although the project manager is responsible for its production it has to be a team activity."

17. Using the Work Breakdown Structure (WBS) to assist estimating is known as:

A. Comparative estimating.
B. Bottom-up estimating.
C. Definitive estimating.
D. Parametric estimating.

> See page 39, paragraph 4.8.1. "Bottom Up Estimating-This method is based on the WBS"

18. People interested in or affected by a project are called:

A. Bystanders
B. Key players
C. Stakeholders
D. Supporters

> See page 33, paragraph 4.3. "A Stakeholder is defined as any person or body that has an interest in a project or its outcome or is affected by it"

19. Which of the following best defines team work?

A. A group of people communicating effectively with each other
B. A group of people working collaboratively towards a common goal.
C. A group of people sharing a common goal.
D. A group of people working under the same leader

See page 86, paragraph 19.2.1. "".. two or more people who
interact, dynamically, interdependently, and adaptively
toward a common and valued goal/objective/ mission"

20. Which of the following is not a component of quality management?

A. Quality planning
B. Quality control
C. Quality measurement
D. Quality assurance.

See page 74, paragraph 8.1.2 The elements of Project Quality
Management are:-

- Quality Planning
- Quality Assurance
- Quality Control

21. The document that represents the prime means of communicating the project manager's intentions to the stakeholders is the:

A. Monthly project report.
B. Stakeholder management plan
C. Status audit report. It is the pr
D. Project management plan.

See page 36, paragraph 2.4overall responsibil. "It is the
primary document that communicates the project manager's
intentions to the Stakeholders."

22. Which of the following would not be classified as a project risk?

A. This project is outside our normal area of expertise.
B. We might not have sufficient people with the right experience to undertake the project.
C. We always find that initial planning takes longer than we thought.
D. We have never worked in that country before.

Risk means uncertainty. If something is always true then
there is no uncertainty hence it is not a risk.

23. The business case is owned by:

A. The project manager.
B. The programme manager
C. The project sponsor.
D. The project board.

> See page 3, paragraph 4.1.4. "The Sponsor owns the Business Case and has overall responsibility to the CEO for its production and realisation."

24. According to APM which of the following best describes a project issue?

A. A future risk that could have a significant negative impact.
B. A previously unidentified risk.
C. A routine project problem
D. A problem which cannot be resolved by the project manager.

> See page 72, paragraph 7.4 "In the PMBOK APM define an Issue as a problem that cannot be solved by the project manager."

25. Portfolio management is particularly helpful in managing:

A. Multiple interconnecting projects.
B. Resource conflicts.
C. Projects requiring multiple skills.
D. Risks to ongoing operations.

> See page 12, paragraph 1.7.1 "Resource allocation considers the requirements of the entire organisation so that an optimum balance can be made between projects and BAU.

26. Responsibility for producing the project management plan lies with:

A. The project sponsor assisted by the project manager
B. The project manager assisted by the project sponsor.
C. The project manager and assisted by appropriate project team members.
D. The project planner.

> See page 38, paragraph 4.6 "The PM is the overall author of the PMP. However some subsections may be written by specialist team members"

27. Which of the following is true with regard to project quality?

A. Having a quality system will ensure that all products are of the approved standard.
B. Project quality is ultimately the responsibility of people actually doing the work.
C. Quality cannot be achieved just by quality control inspections.
D. Quality will follow if everyone follows the quality system.

```
See page 76, paragraph 8.1.8. "Quality is not something
that is achieved by inspection and correction." The motto
is "Get it right 1st time"
```

28. Which process determines if the quality system is being adhered to?

A. Design reviews
B. Project reviews
C. Quality audits
D. Product testing

```
See page 75, paragraph 8.1.4. "Quality Assurance is
defined as the process of evaluating overall project
performance on a regular basis to provide confidence that
the quality system is being followed and project will
satisfy the relevant quality standards." Quality audit is
a component on Quality Assurance.
```

29. A common acronym for an analysis of project context is:

A. PETAL
B. PASTEL
C. PISTOL
D. PESTLE

```
See page 14, paragraph 1.10
```

30. Which of the following best defines a portfolio?

A. The totality of all the projects, programmes and associated operations within an organisation
B. All projects and programmes within an organisation
C. A set of independent projects under the control of one manager
D. A +C

```
See page 15, paragraph 1.7
```

104

Printed in Great Britain
by Amazon